Nepal: Profile of a Himalayan Kingdom

Leo E. Rose and John T. Scholz

First in a series of short introductions to the countries of Asia, this book provides an analytical overview of Nepal's history, culture and society, economy, government and politics, and international relations. The authors begin with the circumstances that have led to Nepal's great cultural and ethnic diversity and then trace the evolution of common political and social institutions that have contributed to the unification of the country while preserving the cultural distinctiveness of numerous groups.

The national political system that emerged in Nepal in the 1950s remained stable during the modern era of development and has enhanced the country's international position while attracting considerable foreign aid. Nevertheless, the infrastructure necessary for continuous economic growth has not been built; neither has the government's ability to implement public policies, particularly those related to economic development, been impressive. It is still uncertain whether the system can adapt quickly enough to avert the problems emerging internally from rapid population growth and externally from the shifting balance of power in South Asia.

NEPAL

Profile of a
Himalayan Kingdom

NATIONS OF CONTEMPORARY ASIA

Mervyn Adams Seldon
Series Editor

NEPAL
Profile of a
Himalayan Kingdom

Leo E. Rose & John T. Scholz

Westview Press / Boulder, Colorado

Published in 1980 in the United States of America by
Westview Press, Inc.
5500 Central Avenue
Boulder, Colorado 80301
Frederick A. Praeger, Publisher

Library of Congress Cataloging in Publication Data
Rose, Leo E.
Nepal: profile of a Himalayan kingdom.
(Nations of contemporary Asia)
Bibliography: p.
Includes index.
1. Nepal. I. Scholz, John T., joint author. II. Title. III. Series.
DS493.4.R67   954.9'6   79-17857
ISBN 0-89158-651-2

Printed and bound in the United States of America

Contents

Preface

Scholarly research on Nepal by Nepalis and foreigners has vastly expanded both in quantity and quality in the past two decades, and there is now a rich literature upon a wide range of subjects. Much of the research has been concentrated in the areas of history, anthropology, and economics, and the results have been truly impressive. In good measure, this is due to the organizational and supportive roles of such diverse institutions in Nepal as the Research Centre for Nepal and Asian Studies, the Centre for Economic Development and Administration at Tribhuvan University, and such private research organizations as the Regmi Research Project and the Nepal Samskritik Parishad. Recognition should also be given to the intensive efforts made by government departments and foreign aid donors to expand and improve data collection on economic and social subjects essential to most of the research undertaken in the social sciences.

For a variety of reasons, much of the research and writing on Nepal has been rather narrowly focused. Most anthropological studies have taken as their subject matter a particular caste, ethnic, or social group or, less frequently, interactions among several social groups in a particular village or region. In the process the *Nepali* social system, defined in national terms, has received much less attention. The economists have been primarily concerned with economic criteria in their analyses of economic development issues, usually preferring to avoid those tedious social and political factors that inevitably intrude upon an otherwise rational intellectual process. Several invaluable historical studies in both Nepali and Western languages now provide us with useful insights into the establishment and integration of Nepal as a unified political and social system. However, these are rarely extended into the twentieth century.

To date, only a few overview studies have attempted to use the wealth of information now available on Nepal, and it is our hope that this volume will be a contribution in this direction. Although we would be the first to admit that the final product reflects the views and subject priorities of the politically oriented social scientist, we have sought to extend our analysis beyond the narrow boundaries of academic divisions, in the hope of suggesting some novel questions to scholars working within their disciplines.

We have addressed this volume to several different audiences. For the general reader interested in Nepal or in other Asian societies, we have tried to interpret, from a social science perspective, some of the broader and more important trends of development in Nepal's history—the evolution of its social, economic, and political institutions and processes, and its struggle for survival in a difficult and threatening international environment. For the Nepal specialists, we present a synthesis of materials designed to fill the gaps among current research efforts and to suggest a series of working hypotheses from a more comprehensive perspective than can be expected from more specialized studies.

The initial suggestion for this study came from Westview Press, and we want to express our gratitude to Mervyn W. Adams Seldon for her useful advice and comments, occasional gentle prodding, and friendly and supportive role at both the writing and production stages. Obviously, numerous Nepali and other colleagues and friends have made major contributions to our comprehension of Nepal—not always, perhaps, in the way intended—and these dialogues have been most stimulating and crucial to us. His Majesty's Government in Nepal also deserves an expression of appreciation. Although some members of the official establishment would differ with our interpretation of events and processes, they have invariably provided us with a freedom of access and a level of cooperation indicative of a liberal and sophisticated attitude toward research that is rather unusual these days. Finally we would like to thank the Institute of International Studies and the Political Science Department at the University of California, Berkeley, for their assistance, and, in particular, Claudia Scholz for her help in the preparation of the manuscript and, even more, for her patience and tolerance.

Leo E. Rose
John T. Scholz

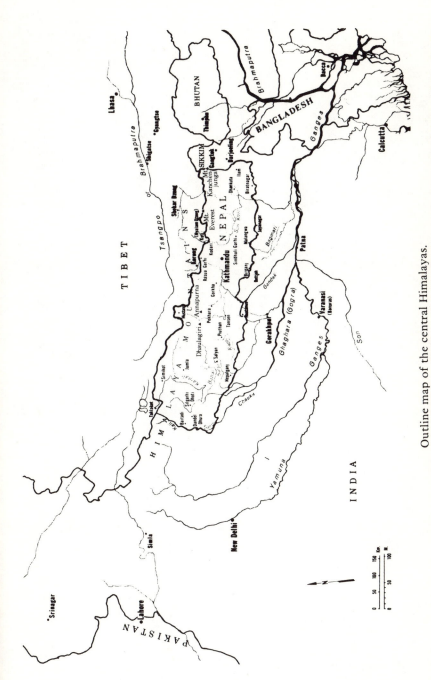

Outline map of the central Himalayas.

Source: Leo E. Rose, *Nepal: Strategy for Survival* (Berkeley and Los Angeles: University of California Press, 1971). Reprinted by permission.

1

Nepal: Environment and History

The Hindu kingdom of Nepal dominates the heartland of the formidable mountain barrier that separates the south Asian subcontinent from central and east Asia. In the hill areas to the east of Nepal lie Sikkim and Bhutan, traditionally centers of a Mahayana Buddhist culture closely related to that of Tibet, the region north of the main Himalayan range. In contrast, the hill areas west of Nepal have long since been absorbed into the Hindu society of the plains area to the south. Nepal, thus, has been the principal arena in which Buddhist and Hindu social and intellectual concepts have interacted in dynamic, sometimes explosive, fashion over the past two millennia. Hindu values and principles have gradually gained ascendancy in much of Nepal; however, they have ultimately emerged from a broad and flexible synthesis with the older Buddhist tradition that is truly unique.

As a unified political and social system, the contemporary nation-state of Nepal is of relatively recent origin, dating back only to the latter decades of the eighteenth century. Indeed, the name "Nepal" was by common usage that of the valley in which the present capital city of Kathmandu is located. It is only in recent decades that the term has come to be applied to the entire country, and even today, for most of the inhabitants of the central Himalayas, to be a "Nepali" is still to be an inhabitant of the Kathmandu valley. Except for a small educated elite with a more assertive national consciousness, citizens of the kingdom usually still identify themselves in regional terms— e.g., Pahari (hill man), Madheshi (plains man)—or by their ethnic

1

community—e.g., Magar, Gurung, Limbu, Rai, Tamang, Sherpa, Tharu, Newar, and so on—at least in their relationships with each other.

The Physical Environment and Traditional Economy

The basic geophysical attributes of the central Himalayas have also contributed to the strong sense of ethnicity that still pervades Nepali society. The southern fringe of the country consists of the outer limits of the great Gangetic plains. This area, known as the Tarai, averages only 10 to 15 miles in width, but runs virtually the entire 500-mile length of Nepal. Until the mid-nineteenth century, most of the Tarai was a densely forested and swampy region most noted for a virulent form of malaria that discouraged habitation. Movement through the Tarai in the hot season (May through October) was extremely dangerous then. Thus, for about half of the year, this potentially productive region constituted an effective deterrent to intercourse with India to the south, as well as to settlement by the Paharis, who considered residence there in the wrong season as a virtual sentence of death. As a result, most of the present inhabitants of the Tarai are descendants either of Indian families who moved in and cleared the land for cultivation during the past century or of local tribal communities that had long been resident there. The integration of both categories of Tarai people into the Pahari-dominated political and social system of Nepal is still not very far advanced. Because the Tarai is the most productive region of the country economically, providing nearly two-thirds of government revenue (other than foreign aid), the potential for separatist movements with accession to India as their objective has been a basic concern of Nepali authorities in Kathmandu.

The hill regions between the Tarai and the Tibetan plateau are extremely complicated geophysically, reinforcing the traditional sense of separate identity among the various hill communities. Three progressively higher mountain ranges (the Siwalik, the Mahabharat, and the Himalaya) intrude on the terrain in an east-west direction while four major river systems (the Karnali, Gandak, Bagmati, and Kosi) run north-south through steep, deep gorges that intersect the mountain ranges, in the process further dividing the hill area into well-defined and distinct regions. Interspersed in these rugged and difficult mountainous areas are several valleys, of which Nepal (Kathmandu) and Pokhara are the most important. The combination of mountain ranges and river systems running in counter directions has made land communication in an east-west direction difficult. The tendency has been for each distinct geographical region to have better-developed communications with either India to the south or Tibet to the north rather than with areas to the east or west. That the Shah dynasty has been able to maintain the integrity of the kingdom under such difficult geopolitical circumstances is a tribute to the ruling elite who have constructed a viable, responsive political system. But the problems of integrating diverse and, in some instances, antagonistic social and regional units into a modern nation-state system are still very real. Only a beginning has been made.

Nepal's mountainous topography and related climatic variations have produced three distinctive types of traditional agricultural economies in the mountain, hill, and Tarai regions, although there is much variation within each of these east-west bands (see p. 4). The cold, sparsely populated Himalayan mountain region to the north supports less than 10 percent of Nepal's population with a pastoral economy based on yak, cattle, and sheep. Many entire villages in the region follow the herds from high-altitude summer pasturelands to winter shelters farther down in the valleys. Although the short summer growing season produces small crops of potatoes, millet, barley, and buckwheat, trading expeditions to sell animal products are necessary to supplement village supplies of food grain. Trans-Himalayan barter trade, exchanging Tibetan salt and wool for Nepali food grain and Indian consumer products, was once an important source of income in this region also. Recently, however, the Chinese have discouraged this trade and restricted access to summer pastures in Tibet, disrupting the traditional bases of the local economies.

In the middle hills, where more than half of Nepal's populace lives, corn, rice, and lesser amounts of wheat and millet are grown on intensively cultivated, carefully terraced fields

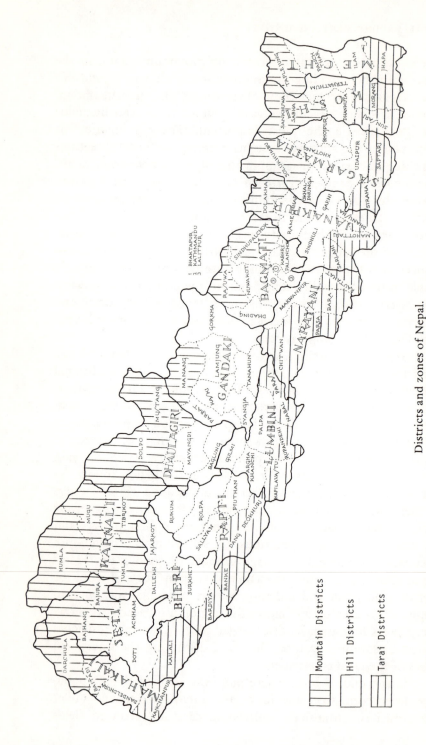

Districts and zones of Nepal.

Source: Bhuwan Lal Joshi and Leo E. Rose, *Democratic Innovations in Nepal: A Case Study of Political Acculturation* (Berkeley and Los Angeles: University of California Press, 1966). Reprinted by permission.

extending from semitropical river valleys to alpine ridges. In most villages, household-scale animal husbandry (cows and draft oxen, goats, sheep, and pigs), home vegetable gardens, and a variety of fruit trees enrich the basic diet of food grain. The primitive transportation system has discouraged the development of any industrial activities (except in the Kathmandu and Pokhara valleys) to supplement the income of hill residents. Some small mining and metalwork operations existed in the seventeenth and eighteenth centuries, primarily for manufacturing weapons for the Nepali army, but most of these operations folded in the nineteenth century when Britain began supplying weapons to Nepal. Household crafts had been well developed in self-sufficient hill villages, although the introduction of textiles and other products from industrial centers in India in the nineteenth century reduced the scope of these traditional activities. Small hill towns have been supported by administrative offices and merchants who import cloth, kerosene, salt, and a variety of foods and consumer goods. To earn cash for these imports and for government taxes, many hill families send their sons to work in India or to serve in the "Gurkha" regiments of the British and Indian armies. Seasonal labor in the Tarai and in India during the winter also helps supplement the supply of food grain in grain deficit areas.

The bountiful Tarai, with its rich alluvial soil, easily farmed flatlands, and abundant forest resources, has developed an export-oriented rice-growing economy more closely integrated with the Indian markets to the south than with the hill economy. About 40 percent of Nepal's populace lives in the Tarai, but they farm more than 65 percent of the country's cultivated land. Surplus rice and jute are exported, whereas corn, wheat, sugar, tobacco, and oilseeds (primarily mustard) are produced primarily for domestic consumption. Forest clearing and logging operations provide alternate sources of employment, as do the growing commercial and small industrial operations in the Tarai towns; but even in the Tarai, agriculture remains the major source of employment.

Agricultural activities vary with the changing seasons. Beginning in April, early rice and jute crops are planted in irrigated fields—lakes, streams, and underground springs provide water for more than 10 percent of Nepal's 5.4 million acres of cultivated land during the wet season, although the irrigation is frequently insufficient for dry-season crops. Corn and millet are planted in unirrigated fields during the same season, when temperatures in the Tarai frequently reach 100 degrees Fahrenheit. Preparation of rice fields for the main crop begins with the sporadic rains of April and May, reaching a peak as the heavy monsoon rains of June provide enough water for the necessary flooding of the fields. Due to the sixty to ninety inches of annual precipitation that occurs primarily during the rice-growing season, 80 percent of the Tarai fields and 35 percent of the hill fields produce this crop.

As the heavy rains taper off in September, the early crops are harvested and a winter crop of mustard or wheat is planted on about 15 percent of the land. By November the main rice harvest begins, and threshing operations are performed during the cool, dry winter months when daytime temperatures are pleasant and nighttime temperatures dip below freezing in the hills. In most areas the climate would permit an annual rotation of two or three crops if sufficient water were available. At present 40 to 70 percent of the fields in various hill districts support two crops annually, while only 15 to 30 percent of the fields in different Tarai districts are double-cropped. Improved irrigation facilities would probably encourage more farmers to intensify their crop rotations and increase the productivity of the agricultural economy.

The Cultural Mosaic: Art, Architecture, and Literature

The interaction of a variety of cultural and intellectual influences originating in India (and occasionally in Tibet) is vividly apparent in all aspects of Nepali culture over at least two millennia. Equally impressive, however, is the skill and devotion with which the peoples of the central Himalayas have absorbed, adjusted, and redefined these external sources of inspiration into cultural patterns that are distinctly their own. In art and architecture, as in the religious traditions that have inspired virtually all the artistic themes and subjects in Nepal, creativity and receptiveness to new ideas are a part of the Nepali tradition.

The critical role of the Kathmandu valley Newar community must be noted, for much of what is called Nepali art and architecture is the handiwork of Newar artisan families who have been practicing their professions for at least several hundred years. The massive and at times brilliant stone sculptures in the Nepal Tarai, which date from the fourth century B.C. to the eighth or ninth century A.D., were the products of prospering local principalities that were an integral part of the Gangetic plains civilization of India. Thus they are Nepali only in terms of contemporary national boundaries. The hill areas, for the most part, were never noted for their artistic accomplishments. The Hindu temples in the mid-hills and the Buddhist monasteries in the north are of interest architecturally and often contain paintings and sculptures of some artistic merit, but they are usually borrowed art forms or acquired possessions rather than the work of local artisans.

Although the history of the Kathmandu valley before the fifth century A.D. is still largely conjectural, there are some impressive architectural accomplishments that, according to local lore, date back to earlier periods. The five stupas (sacred mounds of earth covered with a white stuccolike compound) in Patan and the stupa at Bodhnath reportedly date back to the third century B.C., when Buddhism was introduced into the valley from India. Possibly nearly as old, but Hindu in origin and inspiration, is the temple dedicated to Shiva at Pashupatinath on the outskirts of the present city of Kathmandu. These structures have all been renovated and embellished on numerous occasions in succeeding centuries, but the basic format associated with the Ashokan period in India is still readily apparent.

Architecture in the Kathmandu valley is most noted for its use of the pagoda style, which reportedly antedates the use of this style in China; indeed, it has been claimed that the pagoda style was brought from Nepal to China, though how and when this occurred has never been documented. A few stone temples obviously modeled after those of India are also found in the valley, the oldest of which is located at Pashupatinath. Architectural eclecticism is also evident in the neo-Victorian palaces built by the Rana rulers of Nepal in the late nineteenth and early twentieth centuries. Although not architectural master-pieces, some do have a charm of their own that, unfortunately, is almost wholly lacking in what is called modern architecture in Nepal. There are a few exceptions—the Centre for Economic Development and Administration (CEDA) building on the Trib-huvan University campus in Kirtipur and the high school in the Pokhara valley—but concrete blocks are the general rule these days.

The early art of the Nepal valley is now largely known through the numerous stone sculptures and elaborately designed inscriptions that are associated with the Licchavi dynasty from the fifth to the ninth century A.D. It is probable that elaborate wood carvings were also an integral part of the architecture of the Licchavis (one Chinese visitor wrote with awe about the beauty of the wood architecture in the valley), but none has survived. The stonework is both Hindu and Buddhist in inspira-tion, but both are heavily influenced by the Gupta school of stone sculpturing in India. The principal subjects are the stone lingams of the Hindu Shaivite (Shiva devotees) sect and the various manifestations of Vishnu of the Hindu Vaishnite sect, as well as the Buddha and other figures associated with the Buddhist school of India.

By the fourteenth century, stone sculpturing had almost disappeared in the valley and was replaced by bronze casting and wood carving as the major activity of Newar artisans. Bronze castings may have started as early as the ninth century but began to flourish two or three hundred years later. Although the artisan families who worked in bronze were (and still mostly are) Newar Buddhists, the motifs are both Hindu and Buddhist. Indeed, certain bronzes graphically depict the interaction of Hindu and Buddhist cultures in the Nepal valley. Some portray both Hindu and Buddhist deities on an equal basis, while a number show either a Hindu figure trampling on a Buddhist or vice versa. In these latter cases, the artisan was presumably making a political as well as an artistic statement, probably at the behest of the benefactor or patron who had ordered the bronze.

The dominant influences in bronze works were the Gupta and, much more heavily, the Pala schools of India, although a

distinctive Nepali rhythm and grace in the better examples
make them something more than a reproduction of Indian art.
In the seventeenth and eighteenth centuries, Tibetan themes
(e.g., more Mongoloid features) became common; bronze workers from Nepal valley had been brought into Tibet as early as
the twelfth century, and most of the bronzes usually identified
as "Tibetan" were actually the product of Newar artisans. It
is probable that a steady interchange existed between the
bronze-working families in Nepal and in Tibet, as well as a
profitable export of bronze art to Tibetan religious centers and
noble families. This would account for the "Tibetanization"
of bronze work in Nepal, since there is virtually no other evidence of an inflow of other forms of Tibetan art in the valley
during this period.

Newar skill in wood carving over several centuries strikes
any visitor to the Kathmandu valley, both in the magnificent
temples that abound throughout the valley and the exquisitely
carved wooden windows in the older palaces and homes. The
subjects again are both Hindu and Buddhist, but the styles seem
to be intrinsically Nepali rather than the result of any outside
influence. In the twentieth century, as Nepal set out to
"modernize" itself, both wood-carving and bronze-casting
artisan families found very limited markets for their products,
and at one point it seemed that these crafts would soon dis-
appear. The combination of a revival in Nepali culture and a
growing influx of tourists interested in traditional Nepali arts,
however, has revived the financial fortunes of these artisans.
Although the tourist market has encouraged rapid production
of relatively crude and inexpensive figures, some bronzes and
wood carvings made today compare well with the works of
earlier periods.

No painter caste group similar to those for bronze and
wood carving exists today in the Nepal valley, but there are
some fine examples of Nepali paintings still extant. The earliest
known paintings are illustrations on palm leaf manuscripts,
some of which date back to the eleventh century A.D. A number of murals from the middle Malla period (fifteenth century
and later) have also been discovered recently. The best-known
paintings are the panbhas—paintings on cloth similar to the

Tibetan tankas—which date back to the mid-fifteenth century. The inspiration is obviously Tibetan Buddhist in most panbhas, but there is a distinctive Newar style and form. Influences from India, primarily from the Rajput and Moghul schools, are also noticeable in paintings found in some Hindu temples and in the palaces of the Malla and Shah rulers. A number of contemporary Nepali artists have been trained in India and Europe, but nothing like a Nepali school of modern art has yet emerged.

The literary tradition in Nepal, like that of the arts, is very old and has gone through a series of transformations in language used and in subject matter. The oldest known works are Sanskrit manuscripts of the classic Hindu texts, as well as Sanskrit stone inscriptions from the Licchavi and early Malla periods. From about the fourteenth to the eighteenth century, both Sanskrit and Newari languages were used, but more for religious texts and vamsavalis (family histories) than for literary purposes. After 1770, Nepali began to emerge as the language of literary expression, primarily in the form of poetry, and it also eventually replaced Sanskrit as the medium for official records. Bhanubhakta Acharya, an early poet, is usually given credit for the development of Nepali as a literary language; in the great poetic tradition that has thrived in Nepal ever since, virtually all those with any education, including the most staid of bureaucrats, try their hand at poetic expression at some point in their lives.

Other forms of literature have not developed as far, although short stories, dramas, and even an occasional novel are produced. B. P. Koirala, the noted political leader, is credited with introducing some modern themes—psychology and sex—into Nepali literature. The short story continues to be a medium for subtly disguised social and political commentary. There has also been an attempt to encourage both Newari and Hindi literature—the former in the Kathmandu valley and the latter in the Tarai—but they have not yet made much progress. Once again, Nepal is very receptive to a wide stream of external influences, and constant experimentation with themes and styles can be found in its contemporary literature.

Prehistory and Early History

The area now known as Nepal figures prominently in several of the ancient Hindu classics such as the Ramayana and Mahabharata, suggesting that the central Himalayas had a close relationship with the Indoaryan societies of northern India at least 2,500 years ago. Lumbini, the birthplace of Gautama Buddha in the Nepal Tarai, and the Nepal valley also figure prominently in Buddhist lore. Nonetheless, a coherent dynastic history for the Nepal valley area becomes possible, if still with large gaps, only with the rise of the Licchavi dynasty in the fourth or fifth century A.D. According to some oral traditions, the Kirati dynasties that had ruled the valley earlier were of Kshatriya (ruler and warrior) caste status, but it is probable that the Licchavis were the first Nepali dynasty of Indian (i.e., plains) origin. In any case, the Licchavis provided the precedent for what became the norm in both the Nepal valley and the central Himalayan hills thereafter—the rule of Hindu kings claiming high-caste Indian origin over populations that included large non-Indoaryan and non-Hindu elements. Indeed, it was only with the Muslim invasions of the subcontinent from the eleventh to the sixteenth century that large-scale migrations from the plains into the hills occurred, gradually transforming the ethnic composition of all but the northern fringe of the central Himalayas in the process.

The Licchavi dynastic chronicles, supplemented by numerous stone inscriptions, are particularly full for the period from 500 to 700 A.D. At this time, a powerful unified kingdom emerged in Tibet and established its authority over large areas of central Asia; southwestern China; parts of Ladakh, Sikkim, and Bhutan to the south of the Himalayas; and, according to Tibetan (but not Nepali) traditions, over the Nepal valley. The Himalayan passes to the north of the valley were opened and extensive cultural, trade, and political relations were established. In the process Nepal was transformed from a relatively remote backwater into *the* major intellectual and commercial entrepôt between south and central Asia. As a result, it played a very prominent role in the spread of Buddhist culture, which eventually came to dominate the entire area to the north of the Himalayas. Ironically, this became a divisive factor in Nepal-Tibet relations: in later centuries Nepal was increasingly "Hinduized," while Tibet retained its Buddhist character.

During the Licchavi period, the hill areas to the east and west of the Nepal valley were also undergoing a significant process of change. The stone inscriptions at times describe various Licchavi kings as rulers over vast domains, but in fact their authority was usually limited to the valley and to the trade routes between India and Tibet, which were vital to their economic affluence. Although the dates are still uncertain, it was probably in this period that a number of ethnic communities such as the Limbus in eastern Nepal, various Tibetan groups in the north, the Magars and Gurungs in the central-western hills, and the Khasas in the far west established themselves in various areas of what is now Nepal. All of these communities except the Khasas had tribal cultures that were more closely related, economically and culturally, to the Buddhist north than to India or to the Nepal valley. These groups still constitute a majority of Nepal's population today.

The Medieval Period

In Nepali historiography, the medieval period is usually considered to be coterminous with the rule of the Malla dynasty (the eleventh to the eighteenth century) in the valley. The precise origin of the Mallas is still a subject of debate in Nepal, but there is general agreement that they, like the Licchavis before them, were Indian by descent and high-caste Hindu by self-identification. Most of the Licchavi rulers had been devout Hindus; nevertheless, they had exercised a judicious restraint in seeking to impose high-caste Hindu social codes and practices on their largely Buddhist subjects. The Mallas apparently perceived their responsibilities and opportunities quite differently. Early in the fifteenth century, the great ruler Jaya Sthiti Malla introduced the first legal and social code strongly imbued with Brahmanic Hindu principles in the central Himalayas. Under this code, the Newar community in the valley, which then had a large Buddhist majority, was subdivided into numerous subcastes (jatis) that were strictly enjoined to apply Hindu concepts of social interaction. This constituted a vital step in the ongoing "Sanskritization" (i.e., the process by which low-caste or non-Hindu communities gradually adopt the rituals and ideology of high-caste Hindus) of the Newars. Even more important perhaps, it provided a model for other high-caste Hindu rulers in the hill areas outside the valley, many of whom also ruled over largely non-Hindu populations.

Northern India constituted a potentially serious problem for the Mallas; the history of that area during much of the Malla dynasty in Nepal was one of constant upheaval and warfare. In the eleventh century, repeated Muslim invasions began to spread across the subcontinent from the northwest, culminating in the establishment of the Moghul Empire throughout most of the subcontinent south of the Himalayas. But with the exception of one very destructive, if short-term, Muslim assault on the Nepal valley in the early thirteenth century, the Mallas were not directly involved in these Indian wars. Both the valley and the numerous small principalities in the central Himalayan hills managed to maintain their independence throughout this period.

There was, to be sure, some superficial evidence of Muslim cultural influence in the hills, such as the adoption of Moghul titles and, in name if not in form, land-tenure systems. But the entire Himalayan area to the east of the Kashmir valley proved impervious to efforts at Islamic proselytization and cultural imperialism, managing somehow to keep its Hindu and Buddhist character intact—an important factor in the subsequent history of contemporary Nepal. Although the ruling elite in most of the hill principalities identified very strongly with the Hindu society of India, they rejected the authority and ideology of the Muslim-dominated political system to the south. That the Moghuls were succeeded by equally alien British rulers further reinforced this tendency of the central Himalayan elite to identify with India culturally but not politically. Eventually, indeed, some of them came to look upon the Hinduism of India as polluted by contact with Muslim and British rulers and values, seeing Nepal as the only remaining repository of orthodox Hindu principles and practices.

During the Malla period in the Nepal valley, some basic

political and social changes began to take place in the hill areas to the south and west. The Muslim invasions of India and the destruction of numerous Hindu principalities that followed led to a novel kind of mass migration into the central Himalayas. Previously, most immigrants to this region had been members of communities at a tribal level of political and social organization. Their primary concern was to reestablish the traditional structure of their communities in a more protected and secure environment. The wave of new immigrants, in contrast, was from the elite of the far more complex Indoaryan political systems of northern India. Many were of high-caste status—Brahmans and Kshatriyas—and hence the products of an advanced and sophisticated intellectual and social tradition. Their objective was not to establish a new homogeneous community in the hills but rather to assert their traditional leadership and dominance over the tribal communities that were already there. They were successful in this endeavor, in part through conquest, but largely it seems through intermarriage with and the gradual absorption of the existing hill tribal elite. In any case, by the fifteenth century most of the hill area to the west and south of the Nepal valley was ruled by dynasties claiming Rajput—that is, Kshatriya—caste status, assisted by Brahman preceptors and advisers. Only the Tibetan-populated high hill areas to the north and the Limbu and Kirati regions to the east of the valley managed to maintain the integrity of their traditional tribal communal systems, and even these were not totally unresponsive to Hindu concepts and practices.

One consequence of the introduction of high-caste Hindu elites into the central Himalayan hills was the establishment of two confederations of hill principalities with similar elite structures and diverse populations. The first of these, the Malla kingdom (ruled by a different family than the Mallas of the Nepal valley), was centered in the Karnali River valley; it also controlled the area to the west (Kumaun and Garhwal) as well as adjacent areas of western Tibet across the Himalayan passes. This powerful hill kingdom survived as a unified entity from the eleventh to the fourteenth century. But even after it disintegrated, twenty-two of the principalities in the Karnali region maintained some form of shared identity in what was called the Baisi Confederation. Similarly, there emerged in the area to the west and south of the Nepal valley a loose affiliation of about twenty-four Rajput-ruled principalities known as the Chaubisi Confederation. Although neither the Baisi nor Chaubisi Confederation was an effective alliance system, each did at least project the concept of broader forms of political association among the political elite of the western hill region.

Thus, by the sixteenth century, what is now Nepal was divided into approximately fifty small Rajput-ruled principalities as well as several decentralized tribal polities that were independent or nominally subordinate to one of the Rajput principalities. But more important to the evolving political process in the central Himalayas was the existence of a high-caste Hindu elite with a common political tradition and a sense of cultural identity. This elite, in contrast to the old tribal elites, intermarried extensively across political boundaries, and it was not at all uncommon for a son of one ruling family to ascend the throne in a neighboring state. This helped set the psychological basis for integration into a unified nation-state system. However, the fact that the Nepal valley, the principal political and economic center in the central Himalayas, was ruled by a high-caste Hindu dynasty of different origin from the Rajput ruling families in the western hill areas may well have delayed the unification of the country. As Prithvi Narayan Shah, the progenitor of modern Nepal, correctly perceived, the Nepal valley had to be conquered first before he could move on to the task of absorbing the numerous small principalities his family was interconnected with in so many ways.

Actually, much of the preparation for Prithvi Narayan Shah's conquests had been made by his predecessors, who had established and solidified the rule of the Shah family over the strategically located principality of Gorkha. In the seventeenth century, King Ram Shah had provided Gorkha with the first written legal code in the hill area, based upon the Hindu Shastras but suitably modified to accommodate the social and political traditions of the non-Hindu subjects of the principality. The Ram Shah legal code evoked a positive response not only in his own domain but also in other hill principalities, making the prospect of unification under the Shahs more readily acceptable to both the elites and the populace of the surrounding hill states.

Nevertheless, we must give full credit to Prithvi Narayan Shah's personal contributions to the unification of the central Himalayas into a single state. This remarkable ruler reorganized his armies along lines introduced by the British in India and devised reform programs with more efficient and equitable agricultural system as their objective. Even more important, perhaps, he sought to gain for Gorkha a profitable role in the Indo-Tibetan entrepôt trade by extending his control over trade routes to the north and south of the Nepal valley. Once this had been accomplished the conquest of the valley itself was assured.

The Tibetan government at Lhasa and British officials in India were very concerned with these developments in the central Himalayas for they threatened important and profitable economic relations that both sides were interested in expanding. The British even launched an abortive military campaign in the 1767 monsoon season to maintain Malla rule in the Nepal valley and to reopen the trade routes to Tibet. The Mallas, meanwhile, had been weakened by intrafamilial dissension and widespread social and economic discontent due to the interruption of trade connections with India and Tibet. As a result, the Malla dynasty collapsed rather suddenly once Prithvi Narayan Shah launched an all-out assault on the valley.

Creating a Unified State, 1770-1950

Following the conquest of the Kathmandu valley and the surrounding territories that were under Malla jurisdiction in 1769, the Shah dynasty of Gorkha embarked upon an exercise in imperial expansion never before witnessed in the Himalayan region. Gorkha's armies struck out in all directions on a seemingly haphazard and expedient basis. But although opportunities were rarely ignored, certain basic political and economic considerations preoccupied the new ruling elite in Kathmandu. In particular, mid-eighteenth-century developments to the north and south of the central Himalayan hill area were important to Shah dynasty decision making, for at this time the British East India Company (the "Company") was establishing its control

over northern India from Banaras to Assam, and the vigorous
Ch'ing dynasty in China was resolutely seeking to give substance
to its claim to suzerainty over Tibet.

In Kathmandu the British and the Chinese were perceived
as obstacles to Gorkha's expansionist programs, as well as
potential threats to the existence of the kingdom. Accordingly,
Nepal's policies were directed at achieving several vital political
and economic objectives. The first and most important of these
was a carefully orchestrated effort to bring the more important
trade routes between India and Tibet under Shah control, thus
inheriting the very valuable entrepôt role the Malla kings had
played in trans-Himalayan trade, and at the same time limiting
both British and Chinese access to the hill regions. This supplemented the strongly held view in Kathmandu and elsewhere
in the hill areas that a unified hill state was required to contend
successfully with both British and Chinese imperialism.

Within two decades of the conquest of Kathmandu, the
Gorkhas had achieved their basic objectives. A unified kingdom
controlling the entire central Himalayas from Sikkim in the east
to the Karnali region in the west had been established. In the
process, the trade routes that were then of greatest importance
to the Indo-Tibetan trade were brought under Kathmandu's
control. Some Company officials in India found this irksome,
for they entertained exaggerated notions about the potential
value of the trade with Tibet, and even more important, about
the possibility of trading through Nepal and Tibet with areas of
western China then inaccessible to British commercial interests.
Thus the Company sought to open alternative trade routes to
Tibet, chiefly through a very reluctant Bhutan, but with no lasting success. The Shah rulers did not benefit nearly as much as
they had hoped from their interdiction of the trade routes, primarily because they were a bit too greedy and refused to concede, as the Mallas had done, a profitable role for both Indian
and Tibetan traders in the entrepôt trade. The result was a substantial decline in trans-Himalayan trade for nearly a half-
century, until a more pragmatic government in Kathmandu
finally accepted the necessity for sharing the wealth with non-
Nepali trading interests.

The strategy employed by the Gorkha dynasty in its expansionist programs depended, in most cases, upon the responses of the other hill principalities to this new political entity centered in the Nepal valley. Several of the principalities accepted the inevitable and offered their submission to the Shahs on the best terms they could extract. The ruling families in such areas retained a broad degree of autonomous control over their subjects on internal matters, but had to recognize the Shah dynasty's right to interfere on some issues (e.g., revenue collection and court cases) as well as its sovereignty in the realm of foreign relations. The authority of these local chiefdoms (or rajyas) was gradually eroded over the years by the expansion of the central administration, but it was only in the 1960s that they were finally abolished and their territories integrated into Nepal on the same basis as the other districts. The history of these rajyas reveals important characteristics of the Nepali political system—the patience and care with which the national government expanded its influence and control over regions that had alternative ethnic, religious, or historical forms of identification. With only a few exceptions, Kathmandu made subtle distinctions between reality and rhetoric on vital integration questions up to the contemporary period.

Quiet submission to the Gorkhas was not the path followed by all principalities, however. Some resisted absorption into the Shah polity, either alone or in alliance with neighboring states. The former were doomed from the beginning. The latter on some occasions had substantial military resources at their command, but they usually lacked the capacity to develop effective working relations with their erstwhile allies. The Gorkhas, operating from a secure unified base, played skillfully upon divisions and disputes within the opposition alliances before finally launching an assault. It was not always an easy triumph, and there were a few setbacks, but the Gorkhas would return to the attack after strengthening their forces. The alliance systems, which usually started to disintegrate the day they were formed, eventually collapsed completely. The local ruling families in these states were usually eliminated or forced to flee to British protection in the plains. The principalities were brought under direct rule, with governors (later called bada hakims) appointed from Kathmandu. Although there was no formal local autonomy, as existed for the rajyas, the bada hakims had to accept a working relationship with the local landed-elite families. As long as taxes were paid and order maintained, the local elite were conceded a broad range of powers over social and economic policies. But in these districts, as in the rajyas, the central government cautiously extended its influence on such issues as land tenure, the legal code, and certain social customs (e.g., cow slaughter). In these endeavors, Kathmandu was usually sensitive to local opinion, and changes were based upon a modus vivendi with the local elite. The trend, however, was always in the direction of greater centralization and uniformity.

Whereas most of the hill area to the west of Kathmandu had princely polities not unlike that of Gorkha, much of the hill area to the east was inhabited by "tribal" communities—Rais, Limbus, Sherpas—with diffuse, decentralized political systems. Moreover, the high-caste Hindu ruling families claiming plains origin in the west were almost totally absent in the east except in the southern Tarai area. The process used by the Gorkhas to bring such tribal areas under their control has not yet been described in Nepali historical literature. Certainly, force was used on occasion, but more often Kathmandu seems to have depended upon treaty relationships that differed in significant terms from those reached with the rajya states to the west. The best example, perhaps, is that of the Limbu area (Limbuana), the eastern districts bordering on Sikkim. Under the agreement made between the Gorkhas and the regional chieftains (subbas) of the Limbus, each subba was granted status as Kathmandu's representative in his district with a broader range of powers than those given to either the rajyas or the bada hakims. Equally important to the Limbus, these treaties also guaranteed the kipat (communal land ownership) tenure system, which was critical to the integrity of Limbu society and culture.

In these tribal areas, as elsewhere in Nepal over the next 150 years, the general trend of development was toward a gradual expansion of the central government's authority. This authority, however, was on a more restricted basis, at least in Limbuana. The unofficial changes that substantially altered the local Limbu leadership and land-tenure systems had perhaps a greater effect in the area. These changes were due primarily to the settlement of high-caste Hindu—mostly Brahman—families in the eastern hills, some of which possessed considerable economic and technological resources. These non-Limbu families could not acquire land directly in most cases. However, they were allowed to "rent" kipat lands on an indefinite basis that amounted to ownership rights, quite often as repayment for their money-lending services. Gradually a substantial proportion of kipat lands came under non-Limbu ownership, in fact if not in legal form. Because land was the basis for elite status in rural Nepal, the Limbu local leadership ultimately had to share authority and power with this migrant Brahman elite. The central government actively aided and encouraged this development while formally adopting a policy of benign neglect, ignoring in the process at least the spirit if not the letter of the treaties that had brought Limbuana under the Shah dynasty.

Since the 1860s the Tarai has constituted one of the more difficult regions for the Nepali political system. It is the most valuable area of the country economically, but the most resistant to integration into the rest of the system because of its extensive and deep ties with neighboring areas of India. Located on the Indian border, most of its local landed elite (some of whom were established during the British period of control, from 1816–1860) are of plains Indian origin, as are most of the cultivators. Nepal followed its usual policy of establishing an indirect rule system—contracting out revenue collection, the maintenance of order, and other such administrative functions to local zamindars of primarily Indian origin. Although the Tarai and western hill elites shared a common Hindu heritage, their cultural and language traditions differed in significant ways. The Maithili Brahmans from the Tarai, for instance, distrusted the hill Brahmans and their society, with its many nonconformist concessions to tribal customs and local deities. As a general rule, the hill and Tarai elites did not intermarry.

Kathmandu was never very happy with this situation. The local landed elite's loyalty was always in question and their susceptibility to effective control from Kathmandu was limited. But periodic efforts to strengthen the Tarai administrative system in the pre-1950 period were only partially successful.

Even granting large areas of cultivable land in the Tarai to hill elite families had relatively little effect, because these families usually had to depend upon agents and cultivators of Indian origin. The Tarai was probably the most serious failure in the Shah dynasty's policy of integrating highly diverse areas and communities into its political system, but the area was much too important economically and strategically to be either ignored or allowed to secede.

Creating a Political System, 1770–1846

The transfer of the capital from Gorkha to Kathmandu in 1770 was more than just a change in locale; it involved the construction of a new political and administrative system as well as some significant changes in the elite structure throughout the central Himalayas. With the rapid expansion of new territories and the need to finance an ever-expanding military establishment, something more than just a transfer of the Gorkha governmental system was required. The Gorkha system had been based upon interactions between a comparatively intimate elite group (the "six families" or thar ghar) composed of leading elements of the different caste and ethnic groups that made up the population of the principality. Extensive consultation with the thar ghar on any major decision had been an integral part of the political process in Gorkha and was an important factor in the broad-based support extended to the Shah rulers' ambitious programs for change and expansion.

The Shah court in Kathmandu, as it emerged in the late eighteenth century, was very different in composition from that of Gorkha and operated on some novel rules of procedure. Composed exclusively of high-caste Hindu (Kshatriya and Brahman) families, the new courtier class in Kathmandu was much less representative of the population of Nepal than the thar ghar had been of Gorkha. At the outset, the court was dominated by families from Gorkha that had transferred their home bases to Kathmandu. But rather quickly, other high-caste families (but usually not the ruling family) from other principalities absorbed into the Shah kingdom established themselves in Kathmandu. Both eventually lost their ties to the old home and identified with the new "national" elite that dominated the Shah court.

Nepal has usually been defined as an absolute monarchy in theory, but a limited monarchy in practice. Even the former categorization is not exactly accurate, for in the Hindu tradition there are some theoretical limitations on the power of the monarch. The king, as a manifestation of the Hindu deity Vishnu, is obliged to uphold the traditional Hindu precepts that delegate responsibility for decision making on a broad range of issues to social groups (e.g., castes) as a right, not a privilege. But there is no question that the practical limitations on the powers of the monarch have had greater effect, at times transforming the Shah rulers into puppets in their own court.

Perhaps the most serious problem for the king in the post-1770 period was the division within the royal family itself. The king, his two wives (the normal practice up to 1955), their respective sons, and the collateral branches (Choutariyas) of the Shah family tended to work at cross-purposes, making manipulation of the royal family by other elite factions both feasible and rewarding. The susceptibility of the Shah family to divide-and-rule tactics was further enhanced by the fact that a minor was on the throne for most of the period from 1777 to 1840. The processes of government during this period were actually controlled by the regent and/or mukhtiyar (minister) and the alliance of political factions that provided them with a support base.

A consultative body, called the Bharadari (Bharadar = noble), was set up in the post-1770 period and rapidly became a vital institution in the central decision-making process. Membership in the Bharadari was not precisely defined, but its meetings usually included all high government officials as well as the elders of the leading national elite families. The assent of the Bharadars on major policy issues was essential, and winning their approval was often a very delicate process in view of the highly fractionalized character of the national elite and their propensity for confrontational politics.

Thus, in the 1770–1846 period, politics at the central level was largely determined by intense struggles between political factions, most of which were family based. The family was the principal source of identity for the Nepali elite, and loyalty to the family usually superseded such abstract concepts as loyalty to the ruling dynasty or even to the country. Under such a social system, advancing the interests of the family and its members (usually now called nepotism and decried as a pernicious form of corruption) was a social duty.

The identification of family-based factions, however, has never been a simple proposition. In the national elite, there were five principal Bharadar familial contenders for power and office—the Shah family; the Choutariyas; and the Thapa, Basnyat, and Pande families. But, in fact, it was only rarely that any of these constituted an entity; more often they were divided into subfamily groupings. Two Pande factions, for instance, were almost inevitably aligned on opposite sides in any political struggle. A number of other Kshatriya families, such as the Kunwars (later called the Ranas), and some Brahman and Newar families played important roles in court politics, usually as support bases for the principal Bharadar families. Familial alliance systems (chakari) emerged during this period as a normal feature of Nepali politics. In each alliance, several client elite families were affiliated with a faction led by a Bharadar family. Some of these alliances lasted for several generations with only minor changes in composition.

As one would expect from this kind of political environment, stability was most notably absent during much of the period before 1850, and the little that was achieved was largely due to some sort of equilibration among the contending factions. But mutually acceptable working agreements were difficult to achieve and precarious at the best of times. Court politics, thus, was largely conspiratorial in character and marked by an obvious proclivity for violence. Usually, a ruling coalition of factions did not accommodate its opponents in the governing system, but rather eliminated them through assassination or expulsion. The opposition, of course, retaliated in kind; not one of the mukhtiyars who headed the government between 1775 and 1846 died a natural death.

The prominent hill Brahman families who had followed the Shah court to Kathmandu served both as a support base for and as a check upon the royal and Bharadar families. The Brahmans usually fulfilled these functions without extensive direct involvement in politics. (There were some exceptions, but they were generally Brahmans acting as individuals rather than as representatives of their family.) The Brahmans' role as priests and gurus to the royal and Bharadar families, their skill as astrologers (a technological profession roughly equivalent to that of economic planners today, although the astrologers were probably more successful in their predictive capacities), and their virtual monopoly on the state's legal system assured these families of prominent social status and of a backstage, but nonetheless important, voice in the decision-making process.

The Newar elite that had managed the affairs of the Malla courts in the valley prior to 1769 was initially excluded from the Gorkha system. However, this group eventually had to be accommodated. Newars had administrative and economic skills that the Brahmans and Kshatriyas generally lacked, which were badly needed by the rapidly expanding kingdom. It became the norm for Newars to hold a near monopoly on key second-level positions in the central administration, such as confidential secretaries or economic advisers to Kshatriyas in high office. In addition, the Newars were often vital in the decision-making process as an integral part of the communication and data supply systems upon which decisions were based. They were also less conspicuous and, thus, appeared to be less threatening than the Bharadar families. The political power the Newars possessed is clear from one important example: until the early 1970s the administrative posts in the palace secretariat of the Shah kings were the exclusive domain of two Newar families. Although the members of these families kept themselves discretely in the background, they nevertheless wielded substantial influence.

There were also a large number of important regional caste and ethnic elite families, but after 1770 they played only a minor role in court politics at the center. They continued to critically influence district-level politics, however, and held an indirect veto over certain kinds of decisions (e.g., those affecting land-tenure and taxation systems) through their capacity to obstruct and sabotage central-government policies at the implementation stage. In recognition of this, central leaders made it a practice to grant trade monopolies and new lands to supportive local elite families in order to gain their goodwill and cooperation.

The British presence in northern India and its extension into Nepal through the establishment of a Residency in Kathmandu also contributed to factionalism and instability in the Nepali political system. This was not usually the consequence of direct British efforts to "divide and rule"—although there were a few such instances—but rather the result of Nepali factions seeking British support in their internal squabbles. The Kathmandu court was in general divided into pro- and anti-British factions: the former sought to enhance their authority by soliciting support from the British, while the latter played upon anti-British sentiment, which remained very evident in Nepal until the mid-nineteenth century. There were also pro- and anti-Chinese factions, but given the lack of any Chinese capacity to render effective support, they were usually a mirror image of the British factions.

For Nepal to survive as a unified, independent state, some degree of stability was essential. The major participants in the political process recognized this, and efforts were made to encourage stability through some forms of institutional support. Several offices were assigned as the hereditary right of a particular family—e.g., relations with China and Tibet were the prerogative of the Pande family up to the 1840s. This was intended to give factions some stake in the *system* even when not in power themselves. There was an even more ingenious procedure devised in which command over units of the Nepal army, originally the sole prerogative of the mukhtiyar, was divided among certain civil officials, presumably to provide a balance of sorts in the control of military resources. But these contrivances were never very successful in mitigating the impact of confrontational politics except in those periods when one family alliance system was in a position to dominate most civil posts and, hence, control the army. Here again this was accomplished through suppressing the opposition rather than by accommodating it, and periodic upheavals that emasculated the leadership elements of the main contending family systems at the center were not unusual in pre-1846 Nepal.

What is probably most surprising is that the rest of the

country outside of Kathmandu was in general only minimally affected by the near chaos prevailing at times in the royal court. The holder of a state office, and hence of the landholdings in the districts that went with the office, might change frequently, but the system did not. The local elites developed great skill in adjusting to sudden, dramatic changes in Kathmandu; indeed, the weakening of central authority that usually went along with such developments worked to their advantage. Nevertheless, the need was felt at all levels of government for a more responsive and capable constitutional and administrative system, in part to control exploitation by insecure central officials and ambitious local elites. Out of this psychological milieu, the Rana family system emerged. Initially large sections of the elite in Nepal welcomed the Ranas, even though they came to power in the traditional way—through the violent elimination of the opposition at the center and the monopolization of high government posts. The Ranas may not have promised greater participation in the political process or a more equitable distribution of resources—indeed, quite the opposite—but they did provide a greater degree of stability and order than Nepal had enjoyed since 1770, and this was viewed as a gain by most Nepalis, whatever their social position.

The Rana System, 1846–1950

The fall of Bhim Sen Thapa from power in 1837 resulted in a near breakdown in the authority of the central government. A bitter struggle for power preoccupied the attention of the leading elements at the court in Kathmandu. The jockeying for positions and offices among the contending factions reached such proportions and intensity as to lead to near anarchy. This continued for almost ten years before it was finally resolved in a way typical of Nepal during that period—a sudden crisis led to a bloody confrontation, the assassination of many leading officials, and the emergence of a new dominant faction that quickly moved to monopolize its control over the critical institutions of government. The event was the famous Kot (courtyard) Massacre in the old royal palace; the victorious faction was led by Jang Bahadur Kunwar (Rana), the head of what had been a minor Bharadar family in a client status to the Thapas. Jang Bahadur moved swiftly to consolidate his control. Virtually all of the leading members of the Choutariya, Thapa, Pande, and Basnyat families were slaughtered during the Kot Massacre and its immediate aftermath or else forced to flee the country. King Rajendra and the more troublesome of his two queens were allowed to make a "pilgrimage" to Banaras after having granted full powers to Jang Bahadur. While out of the country, Rajendra was deposed and one of his minor sons, Surendra, placed upon the throne. Even the Brahman Raj Guru (royal priest) family lost its hereditary position and was replaced by another Brahman family allied to the Kunwar faction.

All in all, it was a most impressive performance on the part of Jang Bahadur Kunwar, who ruled as an absolute dictator thereafter. His formal legitimation, as well as that of the Kunwar (Rana) family, was established in the royal sanad (order) of 1856 (the honorific title "Rana" was given to Jang Bahadur by King Surendra in 1858 and was subsequently used as the family name by the Kunwars). Under this order, full powers in both domestic and external affairs were placed in the office of the prime minister, and succession to that office was made hereditary in the Rana family. Jang Bahadur was also made maharaja of two small principalities in the western hills on a hereditary basis. This substantially raised the social and caste status of the Ranas and made them eligible under traditional Hindu caste rules for intermarriage with some families, including the royal family, that would previously have found them unacceptable.

The grant of the maharaja/prime minister office to the Rana family on a hereditary basis raised a serious problem for Jang Bahadur—namely, that of devising a succession system. For internal familial reasons (he had seven brothers who were all very ambitious), the primogeniture principle was not politically feasible. He had to accept a system under which members of the family would succeed to the post on the basis of seniority. Hence, a roll of succession was prepared that listed the eligible Ranas and prescribed the official posts each would hold. The number one male was maharaja/prime minister; the number two, mukhtiyar and commander in chief. The next four held the commanding posts in the four military regions of Nepal, as well as the highest remaining civil posts, and so on. This was all quite innovative, but it also had its problems.

Jang Bahadur was greatly concerned with systemic stability and adopted several measures to further this objective. Effective control over the military was an absolute necessity. This was achieved and maintained by the total monopolization of higher military ranks by the Rana subfamily faction dominant at any particular point in time. Neutralization of the royal family was also essential, and several strategies were employed for this purpose. The royal family was effectively isolated and lived under a virtual condition of palace arrest, being allowed to mingle with the elite or the general populace only under careful supervision. In addition, intermarriage between the Shah and Rana families was encouraged as one way of binding together the fortunes of the two families, and the more recent rulers of Nepal have had a good proportion of Rana blood in their veins. The king's power to veto any act of government by refusing to place the royal seal (lal mohur) on the document was ended by the simple expedient of transferring control of the seal to the prime minister. Later, the prime minister concocted his own seal (khadga nishana), which was used for all but the most important documents.

Although the other Bharadar families had been decimated by the events of 1846, they still could not be ignored. For a couple of decades they were subjected to systematic repression and allowed only a limited involvement in the court. Later, through a process of intermarriage and accommodation into the middle levels of the civil and military administration, some Bharadar elements were reconciled to the regime, at least on the surface. But a strong sense of bitterness was retained by these families up to the last days of the Rana regime, and they were at times a troublesome if not threatening force in the country.

Good rapport with the British Indian government was established by Jang Bahadur relatively early in his period in office, primarily through his policy to support the British in their conflicts in India or elsewhere. Ten Nepali regiments were sent to the assistance of the beleaguered British during the 1856 mutiny, a Nepali unit accompanied the British interventionist force in the 1901 Boxer Rebellion in China, and hundreds of thousands of Gurkhas fought for the British during World Wars I and II. The British were always niggardly in their tangible responses to Nepali assistance, seemingly accepting such assistance as their right, but at least they did whatever was necessary to deter both internal and external threats to the Rana regime.

In their governance of Nepal, the Ranas continued and expanded the efforts made by previous regimes to centralize the decision-making process on an ever-expanding range of subjects. As a general rule, hereditary land grants were not bestowed—except to Ranas, of course—in order to provide the center with broader controls over land distribution. The army was brought under more effective control, primarily through the concentration of most units in the Kathmandu valley, where they were under the direct command of the Rana prime minister. All government servants, whether at the central or district level, were made directly responsible to the prime minister; this had been the nominal rule prior to 1846, but it became a reality under the Ranas. In the annual review system (pajani) under which each government servant (other than the Ranas) was assessed every year, reappointment to a post depended as much on loyalty to the Rana system as on any particular skill in the performance of duties.

A gradual, prolonged effort to "modernize" the administration was also undertaken by the Ranas. Rationally based divisions of functions among offices were introduced into the system. New rules and procedures (sawals) were formulated for each department and made applicable to the entire country. There was even a merit system of sorts applied through the annual pajani that was probably as effective as the nominal merit systems in most bureaucracies today. The judicial system was also reorganized and modernized. A written legal code (Muluki Ain) was introduced in 1854 and periodically revised thereafter. Later, regional courts were established with some degree of independence from the administrative institutions. The objective was to standardize court and legal procedures and regulations to the highest degree possible throughout the country without completely subverting the traditional legal customs of Nepal's many ethnic communities. Finally, an effort was made to rationalize and standardize the land-tenure and tax systems, although the regime at times worked at cross-purposes in this respect by their generous land grants to Ranas or affiliated families.

The policies directed at centralization met with some success, but only on a very limited range of subjects. The regional and local elites retained a considerable capacity to manipulate policies and developments along lines that served their vested interests. This rarely involved direct opposition to central policies or officials sent out to the districts, but rather subtle redefinitions of the former and the co-optation of the latter. Any Rana could exact overt subservience from anybody he met in the hinterland as well as demand instant obedience to any direct command. But once he left, things returned to normal. For their part, the Ranas had to treat the local elites with some degree of circumspection, for they could neither be safely ignored nor easily replaced. Thus on the surface Nepal was a highly centralized polity under the Ranas, though in reality effective decentralization remained widespread.

The Ranas have usually been denounced as feudalistic, reactionary, and authoritarian by their many critics, but this is not a very fair assessment of their regime. Authoritarian it was, and blatantly exploitative, without any apologies. But the system was not feudalistic, at least in the European or Marxist definition of this term. Nor was it reactionary for its time—the Ranas probably introduced more programs of change, and with greater effect, than any Nepali government before or since. The real complaints, of course, are that the Ranas did not share the spoils with the other elite families on an equitable basis and specifically rejected certain forms of economic development—e.g., industrialization—that might have benefited the general public. However, such changes, the Ranas feared, would expose Nepal to massive British and Indian penetration. The determination with which the Ranas maintained Nepal's isolationist economic policy, even at some cost to their familial interests, reflected the regime's extreme sensitivity to external forces and influences that it could not easily control.

The Rana regime was, in fact, reasonably responsive to the broad range of foreign and domestic problems that had perplexed the central government for several decades. Three great leaders contributed in different ways to the system. Jang Bahadur (1846–1877), the innovator, devised its legal and administrative foundations. Chandra Shamsher (1901–1929) consolidated the system after a lengthy period of experimentation and inner travail, and Juddha Shamsher (1932–1945) sought to institute some changes (e.g., Nepal's first economic plan), modeled after policies introduced by the British in India or proposed by the Indian nationalist movement.

The challenges to the Rana regime grew increasingly more serious as the internal and external environment changed. The most serious challenges, however, were divisions within the Rana family itself. As the family grew in size and subdivided into numerous subfamily groupings, familial unity against the outside world was difficult to maintain. In particular, the succession issue became more complex as the number of Ranas who could claim a place on the roll expanded. Position on the roll was the primary determinant of the economic and political well-being of the Rana faction. Each prime minister used his prerogatives to revise the roll in such a way as to give his branch of the family certain advantages. This all led eventually, under Chandra Shamsher, to the division of the family into *A, B,* and *C* categories, initially determined by the caste status of the mother and retained thereafter by all members of that subgrouping. Juddha Shamsher carried this division to its logical conclusion in 1934 by barring all but *A* Ranas from the roll of succession. This was logical, at least from the perspective of Nepali social values, but in the long run it was fatal to the regime because it transformed a large number of *C* Ranas (there were very few *B* Ranas) into a potential opposition force. And, indeed, the most serious internal threat to the Rana regime came from the *C* Ranas after 1934.

Although the opposition based upon the other Bharadar families occasionally caused problems, it never really threatened the Rana system. Several elaborate plots involved members of the royal, Choutariya, and Bharadar families, but the army and civil administration maintained their loyalty to the Ranas, who foiled these plots with comparative ease. A new form of opposition politics emerged in the 1920s, largely as a consequence of the exposure of some young Nepalis from upper- and middle-level families to the Indian nationalist movement. The introduction of a Western-style education system in the early twentieth century also resulted in the emergence of a small group of educated dissidents. These movements never amounted to much on their own strength, but their connections with the Indian nationalist movement and its leaders eventually proved very important.

World War II and its aftermath in south Asia—the withdrawal of the British—posed the most serious challenge the Rana regime had yet faced. Hundreds of thousands of Gurkhas who had served in the war returned to Nepal after having undergone the shock of exposure to new cultures and perspectives. The British withdrawal from India removed one of the most important support bases for the Rana regime, and an adequate substitute was not readily available. The external environment became far more hostile and threatening than at any time since the early nineteenth century.

The attitude of the new government of India, led by Prime Minister Nehru, was uncertain. The Indian nationalist movement's ties in Nepal were almost exclusively with the opposition forces. But the new Indian government was also strongly disinclined to encourage instability and change in surrounding areas at a time when it was trying to establish its own political and governmental institutions under extremely difficult conditions. The Rana regime made a determined effort to come to terms with New Delhi by offering India essentially the same kind of services it had previously extended to the British. For example, 10,000 Nepal State Army troops were "loaned" to India in 1948, when the Indian government faced major challenges in both central India (Hyderabad) and the northwest (Kashmir). The Ranas also introduced a new constitutional system in 1948, formulated with the cooperation of Indian advisers. This system was designed to bring the Nepal government structure somewhat more in line with the one emerging in India.

New Delhi took some time in deciding how to respond to

these obvious overtures from the Ranas. Nehru's preference was for the opposition in Nepal, but he had little confidence in its capacity to overthrow the Ranas on its own or to establish a stable and popular government if it should succeed in gaining power. The Indian government's interim decision, thus, was for a limited accommodation with the Ranas, which it hoped would stabilize the situation in the critical frontier state. A treaty was signed between the two governments in 1950. This treaty, in effect, brought Nepal within the security system the Indians were trying to construct for south Asia, without providing the Rana regime with the types of formal guarantees that had been extended by the British.

In the fall of 1950, shortly after the signing of the treaty, the Chinese Communists launched an invasion of Tibet. This unexpected event generated a change in the Indian government's attitude. New Delhi apprehended that the entire geo-strategic situation in the Himalayan region would thenceforth be fundamentally altered and that the Rana regime would be very vulnerable to subversive activities originating in a Communist-dominated Tibet. India therefore initiated a series of developments directed at introducing a popularly based political system in Nepal. The Indian embassy in Kathmandu helped King Tribhuvan to "escape" from Nepal and brought him to New Delhi where his authority could become an alternative to the Rana regime. New Delhi also allowed the Nepali opposition forces based in India to acquire arms and subsequently to launch an armed insurrection from Indian soil, led by a coalition of anti-Rana factions that had formed the Nepali Congress party in Calcutta in early 1950. The Nepali Congress was able to establish several bases in the Tarai and hill areas less accessible from Kathmandu. There were also serious fissures within the Rana family itself once it became evident that India was going to insist on changes.

The negotiations for the resolution of this complex situation were held in New Delhi. Although the king, the Ranas, and the Nepali Congress were the principal participants, the government of India was the ultimate source for all decisions. An agreement was finally reached in early 1951 that was Indian devised and Indian sponsored. It reflected Nehru's preference for a "middle way"—i.e., an approach to problem solving through a gradual process of change rather than an instant upheaval. A Rana was retained as the prime minister under the new government, but with vastly reduced powers and narrower scope for political manipulation. King Tribhuvan was restored to the throne and assigned a critical role in the mediation of disputes within the government. The Nepali Congress party that had led the revolt was brought into the government and given several key ministries and complete freedom to organize itself as a broad-baseed national party. The system was probably unworkable under the best of circumstances, and it collapsed rather quickly. In retrospect, however, any other solution might well have proved even more disruptive without providing the breathing spell Nepal badly needed not only to construct new governmental and political institutions but also to cope with political movements previously unknown to the country. The Rana regime officially ended in 1951, but many aspects of the system they created are still intrinsic to the functioning of the Nepal government today. What occurred in Nepal in 1950–1951 was not a revolution, but the beginning of a long, gradual, and continuing search for viable institutions and processes that meet national requirements while preserving the basic political culture that has evolved over the centuries.

Nepal and Its Neighbors, 1770–1950

Gorkha's expansionist ambitions in the post-1770 period were not limited to the sub-Himalayan hill area; they extended to certain strategic access routes to the north of the main Himalayan range as well. This soon involved the Shah dynasty in a rather indirect and disguised contest with the Ch'ing dynasty in China—through the Dalai Lama–based regime in Lhasa—for a dominant position in the portions of the Tibetan province of Tsang bordering on Nepal. With the collaboration of some anti-Lhasa Tibetan Buddhist forces in Tsang, Nepal launched an invasion of the frontier section of the province in 1788. In order to obtain the withdrawal of the Gorkha forces, Lhasa had to accept a treaty that granted Nepal some territorial concessions in Tsang as well as important commercial concessions in both Tsang and Lhasa.

Peking's concern over these events was no less than that of Lhasa, for Nepal had in effect challenged China's claims to be the protector of the Lhasa regime and the guarantor of Tibet's security. In 1791, following a second Nepali invasion and the capture of the Tsang capital of Shigatse, a powerful Chinese army was dispatched to expel the Gorkhas and reestablish the authority of the Lhasa regime in Tsang. The Chinese force then launched an invasion of Nepal itself, with the destruction of the Shah kingdom as its proclaimed objective. After some initial successes, the Chinese suffered a severe setback in the last major battle of the war. A treaty was then signed between the Chinese commander and the Nepal government that met the minimal demands of both. The Gorkhas had to withdraw entirely from Tibet and surrender any ambitions for a dominant position in the trans-Himalayan border region. But Nepal retained all of its territories to the south of the Himalayas as well as its commercial privileges in Tibet. Moreover, the Gorkhas gained the right to send periodic missions to the court in Peking, thus circumventing both the Tibetan government and the Chinese Amban (Resident) in Lhasa. These direct contacts with Peking were considered very important, potentially at least, in view of Kathmandu's growing perceptions of a British threat to the south.

China's capacity to influence developments in the Himalayan region, however, declined drastically in the latter half of the nineteenth century. There was a temporary and, for the Nepalis, instructive revival of Chinese activity in the 1910–1913 period when Chinese armies invaded Tibet, forced the Dalai Lama to seek refuge in Mongolia, and established for the first time a reasonably effective control over the country. But the disintegration in China following the overthrow of the Ch'ing dynasty in 1911 led to the expulsion of Chinese forces by Tibetan liberation fighters and to Lhasa's declaration of independence. Nepal had maintained the periodic missions to the Ch'ing court up to 1912, but the system was terminated after the overthrow of the dynasty. China did not figure prominently in Kathmandu's decision making on regional issues (despite a couple of unofficial contacts with the Kuomintang regime in the 1930s) until after Chinese armies once again swept into Tibet in 1951.

Another major objective of Gorkha expansionism in the post-1770 period was the hill area to the west of the Karnali River system, with the distant Kashmir valley as the ultimate objective. This campaign met with rather remarkable success, given the distance from Kathmandu, until it reached the Kangra valley to the north of the Punjab in 1808. The local ruler was on the verge of offering submission to the Shah dynasty when the powerful Sikh kingdom in the Punjab, led by the renowned Ranjit Singh, decided to intervene in support of Kangra. The Sikhs did not want a unified hill state in the territory to the north of their domain, particularly one that would compete with them for control of Kashmir. Kathmandu made the sensible decision not to challenge the Sikhs in an area where they held most of the advantages; an agreement was reached between the two sides under which the Shah dynasty's western border was set at Kangra.

Gorkha expansionism in the post-1770 period was remarkable for its scope and for the Gorkha's willingness to take risks. There is little doubt that the most dangerous exercise in expansion involved the Tarai areas of the Gangetic plains at the foot of the hills, for this brought Kathmandu into conflict with the British who, unlike the Chinese, did have the capacity to conquer and absorb Nepal into their growing empire. Some of these Tarai lands had been under the effective control of hill principalities absorbed into the Gorkha kingdom, and the Shah rulers used this as a basis for their claims to these rich rice lands that yielded considerable governmental revenue. In most cases, however, the hill rulers had held these lands on some form of tributary basis to various Indian ruling families. The British successors to the Indian rulers were not prepared to concede Gorkha's claim to sovereignty over these Tarai lands and insisted that the Shahs accept some form of tributary relationship to the British East India Company in exchange for their use.

Such demands constituted a major theme in Nepali-British disputes during the 1780-1814 period and in the 1814–1816 war. More important to the outbreak of hostilities, however, was British distress over the emergence of a powerful hill state with demonstrated military capabilities astride their very vulnerable and strategic communication lines in northern India. The Company finally decided that it was necessary to take strong action to limit both the power and the territory of the Shah kingdom, with the objective of rendering it dependent on the British. The Company launched an aggressive war against Nepal in 1814, using minor disputes over some Tarai lands as the pretext. The British met with a series of setbacks initially, which left them with a lasting respect for Nepali military capabilities. But eventually the Company was able to gather sufficient military resources to gain a decisive victory over the Gorkhas and to threaten Kathmandu itself. The Shahs accepted the terms offered by Calcutta rather than face the ignominious loss of their capital, which might well have led to the disintegration of the entire Nepali political system.

Under the terms of settlement imposed on Nepal, the Shah dynasty lost all of its Tarai lands to the south as well as the hill areas to the west of the Kali River, Nepal's present western border. In the east, the British restored the small principality of Sikkim, most of which had been conquered by the Gorkhas in the 1780s, and guaranteed it against any form of Nepali intervention. Finally, the Shah dynasty had to accept the establishment of a British Residency in Kathmandu, with undefined but foreboding terms of reference as far as the Nepali elite was concerned.

The 1814–1816 war was a bitter lesson for Nepal, and it was some time before the proud warrior-caste elite in the kingdom was finally prepared to accept the end of the expansion era. But the war had also been a lesson for the British, who discovered how difficult it was to contend with the militant Nepalis on their own terrain. They concluded that Nepal would be even more difficult to govern and from that time on dispensed with any serious notion of bringing the mountain kingdom within their Indian empire. Instead, Nepal became a valued part of the buffer area between British India and China. British-Nepali relations were not always harmonious, but each treated the other with respect and circumspection. In 1856, when British rule in India seemed threatened by the wide-scale "mutiny" in northern and central India, Nepal provided military assistance to the British despite rather strong sympathy among many of the Nepali elite for their Hindu (but not Muslim) brethren involved in the revolt. Kathmandu was rewarded for its efforts by the restoration of most of the Tarai lands surrendered in the 1816 treaty, and in other less tangible ways as well.

With the restoration of the Tarai lands to Nepal in 1860, the present national boundaries of the country were settled. Also in the post-1860 period, the terms of Nepali-British relations, vital to Nepal and important to the British, were set in reasonably precise formulas. A modus vivendi basically satisfactory to both governments was achieved. The British agreed not to intervene in Nepal's internal politics and economy and also to respect Kathmandu's isolation policy, which barred British access to areas of Nepal other than Kathmandu and certain transit points in the Tarai. Even the British representative in Kathmandu was restricted to the valley and never enjoyed the kinds of influence and power his colleagues wielded in the Indian princely states. In exchange, the Nepalis generally accepted British "guidance" on Nepal's external relations in what amounted to a limited subordinate status in the British Indian frontier security system. The British also gained the right to recruit Gurkhas for their Indian army, which became an increasingly important source of support for the British as the Indian nationalist movement gained in strength and capacity in the early twentieth century. The Gurkha regiments came to be viewed as the best and, more important, the most reliable units in the British Indian army and were often used in confrontations with Indian political movements in preference to Indian or even British forces. Nepal also benefited from the recruitment system: economically they prospered from the earnings, pensions, and knowledge that returning soldiers brought into overpopulated and underdeveloped hill areas; politically they gained ground due to the fact that increasing dependence upon the Gurkhas raised Nepal's value to the British and, hence, increased its bargaining power with British India.

The point to note here is that by the latter quarter of the nineteenth century Nepal's status as an independent state, with some irksome but largely nominal limitations on its external relations, had become intrinsic to the Nepali-British relationship. A treaty signed in 1924 formally recognized Nepal as an independent state, but this only made de jure what was already a de facto situation. Critics of the Rana family political system that ruled Nepal in this period have made its supposed dependency on British India a major point of criticism. But in retrospect, given the extremely unfavorable geopolitical environment in which the Kathmandu government had to operate during most of this period and the lack of any alternative external source of support, a good argument can be made that the Ranas were remarkably successful in maintaining a broadly defined and respected autonomy for Nepal while preserving its cherished cultural and social values against insidious external influences then widely prevalent in India.

2

Building a Modern Political System

The collapse of the Rana regime in 1950 cleared the way for some basic changes in political institutions and processes in Nepal. In three short decades, the political activities of new groups previously suppressed or ignored by the Ranas were accommodated while political and administrative institutions were reorganized to include the standard patterns expected in modernizing nations. By the mid-1970s, Nepal had "representative" institutions at the local and national level, a cabinet led by a prime minister, a system of courts and a modern code of law, an organized cadre of civil servants, and, of course, a planning commission. The absorption of new groups, particularly local notables and village elites, into these expanding central institutions coincided with the expansion of the development tasks of the government and the penetration of bureaucratic authority into new activities previously controlled by local elites.

Yet despite considerable change in the actors, stakes, and institutional framework of political conflicts, the persistence of traditional patterns of interaction gave these modern institutions a uniquely Nepali character. The numerous experiments and changes of the past three decades have not as yet seriously disrupted the basic stability and continuity of the political system. This resilience is a tribute to the political skills of Nepal's leaders. Their skills have not, however, been matched by an ability to design policies and create agencies to successfully implement the development objectives they have professed. But in order to understand these policy failures and to analyze

41

the relative strengths and weaknesses of the present political regime, it is necessary to know more about the issues and forces that have shaped Nepal's political institutions.

King Tribhuvan and Party Politics, 1951–1955

The Delhi Compromise, which created the first post-Rana government, was an agreement between the four major groups that were to dominate Nepali politics throughout the 1950s: the monarchy, the political parties, the Ranas, and the Indian government. A rapid succession of weak ministries had to cope with the struggles among these groups over the principles of legitimate rule and the controls of state authority as each succeeding cabinet sought to create the institutions of a modern nation-state. The Interim Government Act of 1951, which established some ground rules for this struggle, exhorted the new leaders to "strive to promote the welfare of the people by securing . . . a social order in which justice—social, economic, and political—shall inform all the institutions of the national life." The act called for limitations on the powers previously held by the Rana prime ministers and for dispersion of the powers necessary for reforms among democratic institutions. Even though the act was a hastily drafted document based on the principles of the Indian constitution and written with the aid of Indian advisers, it did express the aspirations of the new generation of Nepal's political leaders. The problem, of course, was how to create such institutions.

The excitement of creating a new political order was dampened by the more critical task of reestablishing a central authority to replace the Rana system, which had disintegrated during the armed insurrection. Competing parties, particularly the Nepali Congress (which had led the armed insurrection) and the Gorkha Parishad (organized after the Delhi Compromise by high-ranking Ranas as a counter to the Congress threat), had their own private police to protect party leaders and to control political rallies. These private forces did not always obey party leaders—one regional party leader's attempted coup in 1952 almost succeeded in overthrowing the first Nepali Congress cabinet by using the Congress party's own police force! Particularly in the Tarai and in the eastern hills, political turmoil led to agrarian unrest that further exacerbated the general disorder facing the government.

Within this chaotic situation, the Shah dynasty soon proved its resilience when King Tribhuvan emerged as the central figure in the political struggle for leadership. Despite his retiring personality and modest political ambition, Tribhuvan became a hero of the "revolution" overnight; his dramatic flight to the Indian embassy had been instrumental in forcing the Ranas to relinquish power. At the same time, the monarch's status enabled him to interact with the ensconced elites in the bureaucracy and, most importantly, with the army. The Interim Government Act granted Tribhuvan the power to appoint interim cabinets until a representative assembly was elected. But since political maneuvers by disgruntled opposition leaders to discredit appointed ministers weakened the cabinet's effectiveness, the king soon became more directly involved in negotiating specific issues and making necessary government decisions. Several amendments to the Interim Government Act further strengthened his ability to deal directly with law-and-order problems without the approval of other institutions. He devoted considerable attention, particularly after the attempted coup of 1952, to strengthening the army's capacity to deal with disorder and with the military threat of the private police groups. Thus, by September 1954, when ill health forced the king to seek medical treatment in Switzerland (where he died several months later), the monarchy had become the focal point of political negotiations.

King Tribhuvan's position was considerably enhanced by the support he received from the Indian government, which continued to play a major role in the government it had imposed on the other participants. Nepal's political leaders twice traveled to Delhi to settle internal difficulties. In addition, Indian Ambassador C.P.N. Singh functioned as Tribhuvan's political adviser and even intervened directly in policy and political appointment matters. Nepali Congress leaders, who had been socialized into politics through involvement in the Indian nationalist movement, retained close working relationships with their Indian mentors. Even the Ranas sought and accepted

Indian advice and guidance on how to function in the new political system so alien to their whole approach to politics. Technical experts from India were active in reorganizing the Nepali administration and army, and the Indian army itself operated in Nepal on several occasions when the Nepali army was incapable of handling disturbances in the Tarai.

Although Indian leaders sympathized with their counterparts in the Nepali Congress party and had encouraged their opposition to the Ranas, including armed intervention, the party appeared to be too unorganized and too internally divided to set up a stable regime in Kathmandu. The Ranas also appeared to be too divided among themselves with too little popular support to provide the dependable bulwark desired by New Delhi. King Tribhuvan, on the other hand, represented the only popular political force with some potential for moderating conflict among other political elites. Thus, India relied increasingly on Tribhuvan, whose concern for establishing a stable regime and willingness to accept Indian advice in the uncertain political and international context coordinated well with India's needs for flexible responses until its long-term policy interests in Nepal could be clarified. But New Delhi's indiscreet and at times abrasive intervention into political, administrative, and military matters alienated many of Nepal's political and bureaucratic elites, reinforcing Nepal's traditional fear of domination by its southern neighbor. This distrust of Indian motives, particularly by Crown Prince Mahendra (who was soon to ascend to the throne), was to becloud relations between the two countries.

The Ranas lost their official claim to power in 1951 when Tribhuvan˙ revoked all powers granted by previous Shah kings to the Rana prime ministers. The political changes of the 1950s further divided the Rana ranks, with some influential Ranas becoming party organizers while others refused to recognize the legitimacy of any political parties or their reform programs. After 1951, high-ranking Ranas played little part in ministerial politics and several branches of the family went into exile in India. However, despite the reform programs proposed by party leaders to undercut Rana influence, the social prestige, financial resources, and information networks developed before 1950 continued to give the remaining Rana leaders, many from the lower-status C-class Rana families, considerable influence over government activities. Rana families and their clients continued to hold high positions in the bureaucracy and the army, while their traditional controls over various local elites provided a valuable resource under the newly recognized democratic norms.

Party leaders, the newest and most visible element in post-Rana politics, brought with them an influx of elites from all levels of society who wanted to end the Rana political monopoly. Parties appeared to hold the key to future political power as "representatives" of the people, since King Tribhuvan's 1951 proclamation called for the formation of a representative government. But the Rana regime fell too quickly for the principal party, the Nepali Congress, to unite all the anti-Rana factions that had joined the opposition movement. Competition for ministerial appointments and government spoils divided the rudimentary party structure before organizational discipline took hold. Furthermore, the party had difficulty accommodating Kathmandu-based anti-Rana leaders not represented in the exile leadership, who consequently organized their own parties. Finally, a leadership struggle between B. P. Koirala, the party's acknowledged leader, and his half-brother M. P. Koirala, who in 1952 was appointed prime minister by the king (in consultation with the Indians), eventually splintered the party into several factions. Competing party leaders used the new techniques of protest rallies and civil disobedience to discredit governments from which they were excluded. Parties publicly debated their ideological positions, but once in power they were more concerned with using government resources to weaken other parties and strengthen their own organizations.

The structure of these early party organizations reflected the patron-client relationship characteristic of the Rana social order, although there was considerably more variety in party recruitment techniques than Rana patrons had had. Some leaders gathered followers through personal charisma or ideological persuasion; others through previous acquaintances in schools, the British or Indian army, or earlier political activities; still others by extension of more traditional relationships or ethnic identity. Successful party leaders attracted followers

who themselves were patrons with their own following, thus
creating party linkages based on personal support through
several intermediate patrons.

Throughout the 1950s, members of the incumbent prime
minister's party frequently expanded into new geographic areas
as district notables and town and village elites were attracted
by the party's command of state authority and resources.
Loyalty varied considerably in intensity and longevity, with
numerous intermediate patrons shifting their allegiance when
conditions changed. Ethnic identities, status conflicts, and
regional factors, of course, limited the interchangeability of
these intermediaries—if a powerful notable joined one party,
local factions who opposed him would seek the support of a
competing party. On the other hand, a family often had members in competing party organizations, thus improving its
chances of survival despite existing political uncertainties. As a
result, parties developed as a complex mosaic of political support based primarily on personal relationships, many of which
in fact outlasted the parties and continued even under the
panchayat system discussed below.

By the end of Tribhuvan's reign, party leaders controlled
most cabinet positions and dominated public political forums.
As a group, however, they were too divisive, disorganized, and
unrepresentative of the country as a whole to establish a stable,
legitimate regime. Since most important political confrontations
took place in the Kathmandu valley and the Tarai towns, party
mobilization was most intense in these areas. Intellectuals,
financial supporters, and local organizers who could guarantee
large turnouts for political rallies were the most prized recruits
because they provided some semblance of popular support to
strengthen the leader's position in the palace intrigues for ministerial appointments. The national elections King Tribhuvan had
promised would have forced party leaders to broaden their
support base, thereby increasing their "democratic" legitimacy,
but would also have forced Kathmandu-based elites to relinquish their traditional monopoly of positions in central institutions. The small parties and associations organized by these
elites preferred (in private, at least) the system of court intrigue
to elections, which would have favored parties with more extensive contacts in the countryside.

King Mahendra and Party Politics, 1955–1960

When Tribhuvan died in 1955, his son King Mahendra moved assertively to consolidate the central political role of the monarchy. Disgruntled by the arrogance Indian and party leaders had displayed toward the monarchy and by their apparent lack of concern for what he perceived as Nepal's national interest, Mahendra adroitly used the powers that Tribhuvan had gained with the aid of these leaders to weaken their positions in the evolving political order. After experimenting with six different types of cabinets during the first six years of his reign, Mahendra successfully imposed direct rule in 1960, jailing most party leaders and banning political party activities despite ominous Indian threats. But the continuing conflict over political legitimacy throughout the 1950s left little time to enact or implement the major social and economic issues that had been debated in public forums.

Despite the king's concerted efforts to build a broader support base outside Kathmandu, he was unable to compete with party leaders for control of votes in the countryside. Beginning in 1956, King Mahendra undertook extensive tours to meet local leaders throughout the country, dispensing immediate justice, expediting government approvals, and distributing government gratuities. His direct contact with the broad spectrum of Nepal's elites and his shrewd evaluation of their motives became his most valuable political assets. During the same period the Nepali Congress and, to a lesser extent, the Communist and Rana-led Gorkha Parishad parties sensed that court intrigue under Mahendra was unlikely to bring them to power. Consequently, they strengthened their district-level organizations throughout the country. Using recruitment tactics learned from their experience in India, they began building an electoral base to solidify their claim of popular support. At the same time, they aroused public agitation for the national elections King Tribhuvan had promised.

Mahendra attempted to defuse the election issue by catering to smaller parties and associations willing to delay national elections. He also selected his own delegates from politically active groups to represent the government in special conferences and assemblies that he organized to provide a popular facade for his regime. When unified agitation by the major parties could no longer be ignored, Mahendra, in one of his typical surprise moves that kept his political opponents off balance, called for elections to a national parliament—not to the constitutional convention Tribhuvan had promised. Furthermore, the parliament would govern under a constitution that Mahendra himself promulgated. Party leaders reluctantly accepted the king's terms, despite the constitution's generous grant of powers to the king, because they did not want to give Mahendra another excuse for postponing elections. In early 1959, after a remarkable effort by the administration and a specially designated interim cabinet to organize and oversee Nepal's first national election, the Nepali Congress won an unexpected 74 seats from the 109 parliamentary districts. The Gorkha Parishad won in only 19 contests, and other parties fared even worse. Most surprisingly, local notables, some of whom ran as pro-palace independents, won only a few seats. Thus, in July 1959, after some initial hesitation, the king confirmed the parliament's choice of Nepali Congress leader B. P. Koirala as Nepal's first elected prime minister.

Koirala and his associates soon proved to be as adept at building party strength within the framework of the king's constitution as they had been at building the party's electoral base. Despite the ethnic, regional, and ideological differences within the party—similar to the differences among party leaders that Mahendra had manipulated so skillfully—the king was unable to undermine party discipline among Congress parliamentarians. Koirala, on the other hand, strengthened party control over the bureaucracy by promoting Congress supporters to top administrative positions and by forbidding direct contacts between administrative officials and the palace, thereby decreasing the conspiratorial capacities of bureaucrats loyal to the king. In addition, the party appointed its own members to a parallel "development bureaucracy" that channeled development funds directly to the districts, bypassing the controls of entrenched central bureaucrats. Local elites quickly learned the advantages of Congress party membership and swelled the lower ranks of the party. Thus, by 1960 Nepal's political order appeared to be evolving toward a dominant party system similar to the one established by the Indian Congress party in India.

However, established political groups who mistrusted the Tarai-oriented, social-democratic Congress leaders quietly supported a return to the palace-centered politics of the 1950s. Other parties that mistrusted the king and shared the democratic aspirations of the Congress party feared that their supporters would desert them and join Koirala's dominant party. Nor was Mahendra content with the limited political role of a constitutional monarch as envisaged by the Congress leadership. Unable to outmaneuver Prime Minister Koirala within the constitutional framework, the king resorted to the emergency powers granted to him by the constitution. On December 15, 1960, with the support of the army he had carefully nurtured, Mahendra dismissed the cabinet and arrested its leaders, charging that the Congress government had failed to maintain law and order and provide national leadership. The wholesale arrest of leaders from all parties had an inhibiting effect on protests against the royal takeover, but the almost complete lack of public outcry from other groups demonstrated the king's ability to gain at least their acquiescence to his rule. Eighteen months had not been sufficient for the Congress government to build a strong network of support among the important central elites.

Mahendra's Panchayat System, 1961-1972

Nepal's political instability throughout the 1950s, according to the supporters of the new regime, proved that the externally inspired system of parliamentary democracy was not appropriate for Nepal. Consequently, the king promised to introduce a more suitable national political system, based on indigenous village councils (panchayats), that would build democracy "from the grassroots." The panchayat system—which traditionally had never played the supravillage role assigned to it under the new system—eventually provided the institutional basis of Mahendra's rule.

In the immediate aftermath of the royal takeover, the king's conservative bases of support made it appear likely that most reforms enacted by the Congress regime would be rescinded and more traditional institutions would be reactivated. Even

while his father was alive, Mahendra had courted Rana support
by marrying into a Rana family despite Tribhuvan's objections.
Army leaders who played major roles in the royal takeover were
Ranas or Rana allies. Rana-backed conservative and religious
groups rumored to have direct contacts with the palace were
involved in violent disruptions that provided the pretext for
dismissing the Congress government. Palace Brahmans, who
presided at official religious ceremonies (and gave credence to
the tradition that the king was an acclaimed manifestation of
the Hindu god Vishnu) continued to advise the king.

Mahendra was aware, however, that the royal regime's
survival was as dependent on international acceptance as on
internal political support. Leaders of the Nepali Congress, Communist, and Gorkha Parishad parties who had escaped to India
joined forces to mount the same kinds of armed attacks that
had been used against the Rana regime a decade earlier. The
Indian government officially recognized the new regime, but
tacitly supported the opposition groups even to the extent of
imposing a potentially crippling economic boycott on Nepali
trade to force a rapprochement between king and party leaders.

Fearing a return to the chaotic period following the Rana
downfall, Mahendra rejected compromise with Indian and party
leaders and instead sought to win international legitimacy for
his new regime. Ironically, Indian military assistance during the
1950s had improved the Nepal army's ability to maintain law
and order and to counter guerrilla attacks organized by party
leaders from bases in India. While maintaining law and order,
the king attempted to establish a progressive image for his regime
by introducing reforms more extensive than those the Congress
regime had proposed but had been unable to implement. Foreign
aid was sought from all sources to enhance the regime's development credentials and to give aid donors a direct stake in the
survival of the regime. More pointedly, the king sought to use
China's military presence in Tibet to discourage Indian intervention in support of party leaders.

The armed threat posed by party leaders and tacitly supported by India subsided after the short but dramatic Sino-
Indian war of 1962 (fought in other parts of the Himalayas),
but domestic reforms undertaken primarily to impress the in-

ternational audience had by this time proven their utility for
the king's domestic strategy as well. Birta reforms introduced
by the Nepali Congress regime to confiscate large Rana landholdings and diminish private Rana controls over these areas
were implemented even more forcefully by the royal regime.
The major Rana families, after all, represented a viable conservative alternative to Mahendra's direct rule, one that the king
preferred to eliminate. Rajya reform abolished the special
authority and privileges granted to a handful of hereditary
leaders descended from the Rajput ruling elite of medieval
principalities in western Nepal. And a major land-reform program, launched in 1964, was aimed primarily at the powerful
local elites who had continued to support and finance illegal
party activities even after the royal takeover.

These "egalitarian" reforms not only dispersed troublesome concentrations of power but also appealed ideologically
to the young intellectuals, both in and outside the bureaucracy,
who otherwise would have supported the democratic legitimacy
of the political parties. The new legal code introduced in 1963
was written primarily by foreign-trained legal experts who rejected traditional caste principles and emphasized the equality
of rights for all citizens. Similarly, foreign-trained economists
were instrumental in devising and implementing the land-reform
program's tenancy reforms, which were designed to improve the
status and independence of the cultivator. Development programs not only attracted foreign aid but also provided an ideological justification of the royal regime as well as government
jobs for the small but influential number of educated elites.
Furthermore, the beneficiaries of these reforms, particularly the
50,000 to 60,000 representatives in the new panchayat institutions, provided a broad (although not always dependable)
basis of support for the king's rule.

During the first years of the royal regime, Mahendra had
appointed as ministers disgruntled young party leaders who
supposedly could mobilize popular support for the regime
among rural elites and ethnic groups. In addition, the panchayat
system of elected representatives was designed to recruit loyalists
who would oppose party activities on the village level. It also
gave the Council of Ministers (as the cabinet was called for the

first few years of Mahendra's direct rule) an elective facade easily controlled by the palace. Elections to the National Panchayat were indirect, proceeding through a hierarchy of village, district, and zone levels. As originally designed, each of the approximately 4,000 village panchayats directly elected its own mayor (pradhan panch) and vice-mayor, while each of the nine wards within the panchayat elected its own representative to the village council. Each panchayat sent one member to the district assembly, which selected the district chairman, vice-chairman, and nine-member council from among its forty to seventy members (depending on the number of panchayats in the district.) The seventy-five districts were divided into fourteen zones. Members of all district councils in a zone voted for the representatives each district in the zone sent to the National Panchayat. In addition, a parallel system of "class" organizations elected two to four National Panchayat representatives from the women's, peasants', workers', ex-soldiers', and youths' organizations. The Graduates' Constituency enabled the approximately 10,000 Nepalis with college or Sanskrit degrees to elect directly four national representatives. And, finally, the king appointed approximately 20 percent of the National Panchayat members. Ministers were appointed by the king from the National Panchayat.

In addition to the legal ban on party activities, several features of this system weakened the electoral strength of party members. First, members affiliated most closely with the Congress and Gorkha Parishad parties, who expected the Indian-based armed opposition to eliminate the panchayat system, boycotted the initial village panchayat elections in 1962. Armed intervention had already ceased when the indirect national elections took place, but local party leaders who had not contested seats on village panchayats were not eligible for district or national elections. In addition, the Ministry of National Guidance, which supervised panchayat elections, was created primarily to assure that parties did not gain control of the system, although some Communist party members who were willing to support the panchayat system and thus gain an advantage over their Congress opponents entered the system with tacit approval from the palace. Secondly, panchayat members defended their panchayat positions in subsequent elections by blocking, with administrative assistance, the advance of party candidates; due to the small number of electors, a few administrative favors in return for votes could defeat a candidate who had considerable popular appeal. And, finally, the system was designed to favor rural hill elites over the more urban Kathmandu and Tarai elites who had been most active in the parties. Village panchayats vastly outnumbered the few town representatives in district assemblies, whereas zonal assemblies grouped each Tarai district with several hill districts.

Despite the numerous central controls over the system, Mahendra faced considerable difficulty in assuring the continued loyalty of panchayat elites. Many elected panchayat members had at least been associated with the political parties during the 1950s. Ministers in the early cabinets were strong personalities with skills in manipulating policies and the symbols of office to organize their own independent power bases. After India had adopted a more nonpartisan policy and the threat from the parties receded, Mahendra replaced the more independent ministers with weaker, less-sophisticated political leaders whose primary function was to represent the geographic areas and ethnic groups to which they belonged. The carefully balanced Council of Ministers kept panchayat members content by distributing individualistic rewards, but ministers, with a few exceptions, had little influence over general policy issues. Panchayat institutions at all levels were never given the important functions and duties projected in the initial plans. Public attention and debate during the late 1960s focused primarily on the controversial party leaders, several of whom were still in jail, and on their demands that either the panchayat system be abolished or political parties be allowed to contest elections. Some panchayat representatives even declared their party affiliations openly in defiance of the government ban on parties. But the locus of policymaking at all levels had already shifted from the new political elites to bureaucratic elites in the reorganized administrative system.

By the mid-1960s, the administration had changed considerably from the small, well-ordered hierarchy of the Rana era. Political uncertainties had induced increasing instability during the 1950s as political leaders undercut the formal hierarchy to seek out administrative officers whom they could trust. The bureaucracy grew steadily as each new cabinet promoted and appointed its clients to important positions, thus adding partisan divisions to the existing caste cleavages among the Brahmans, Chetris, and Newars who monopolized government service. The rapid advance of young, partisan, educated bureaucrats into positions traditionally reserved for senior members of bureaucratic elite families further divided the bureaucracy.

Mahendra increasingly relied on administrative leaders rather than on political elites to direct government activities and moderate political conflicts for several reasons. Most importantly, individual administrative officers knew that their survival depended on loyalty to the king; Mahendra had twice screened all administrative officers, once upon ascending the throne and again in 1961, when he removed thousands of officials suspected of loyalty to the deposed Congress government. The education, administrative experience, and practical knowledge that top officials had gained about the problems of government contrasted favorably with the brash, ideological orientation of many political leaders. Additionally, bureaucratic elites had several reasons to prefer the royal regime over the Congress party alternative. First, bureaucratic elites gained greater control over government policy, including recruitment and placement, when the weaker panchayat ministers replaced their more powerful party counterparts. Second, the king's ban on party activity guaranteed the bureaucracy's monopoly; it was the only national institution capable of routinely intervening in local affairs throughout the country. Third, administrative officers who had survived the 1961 purge preferred the king's traditional centralist orientation to the parties' decentralized orientation toward the notables and village elites who controlled votes. And finally, the king's reliance on bureaucratic policies to stimulate economic growth expanded the size and resources of the administration as well as the scope of its powers over local elites. Thus a symbiotic relationship developed as the bureaucracy accepted, with some reservations to be sure, the dominant position of the king.

Mahendra employed a strategy of intimidation and planned

institutional conflict to preserve his control over the bureaucracy. Officials were routinely transferred to different posts in
order to weaken their command over their offices; individuals
who fell into royal disfavor were assigned to an unpopular post
or dismissed during these periodic rotations. District-level
authority was hopelessly fragmented between the chief district
officer (who inherited most of the responsibilities of previous
Rana district governors without the prestige or authority),
the elected district panchayat chairman (who had been promised
greater authority, but was powerful only insofar as he commanded political loyalty and could disrupt government activities), and the field officers from central departments (who
directly supervised most development projects in the district).

Similarly, central authority was split among numerous
institutions. The Central Secretariat, which housed all top administrators of secretarial rank, was directly responsible for
implementing policies, and each ministry's secretary retained
considerable control over his portfolio's field offices. But the
"political" cabinet minister was officially superior to the "civil-
service" secretary and retained a certain influence over the implementation of policies, particularly in districts where his
political clients were active. In addition, fourteen commissioners
were responsible for governing the zones. They reported directly
to the palace and were appointed from powerful notable or central elite families that had developed client relationships with
the royal family. These administrators eventually exerted the
most influence within their zones, for they possessed broad
powers over law-and-order issues and indirect controls over panchayat elections. The central institutions thus created such a
maze of overlapping authority, conflicting jurisdictions, and
competing support groups that only direct palace intervention
could cut through the inevitable conflicts and resolve important
policy issues—precisely the result King Mahendra sought in this
carefully constituted institutional balancing act.

The king relied on a few very capable, trusted, and experienced central secretaries to penetrate this institutional maze on
all important policy issues. These secretaries provided a negotiating focal point for groups within the bureaucracy as well as
for outside political elites—even delegations from distant vil-

lage panchayats sought audiences with these secretaries or their associates to discuss local implementation of government programs. By playing one group against another during policy formulation and implementation, the secretaries were able to achieve many of the king's (and their own) objectives while still meeting the demands of groups whose support was important for the survival of the royal regime. In fact, the secretaries extended the use of the manipulative strategies Mahendra himself had perfected. As the secretaries increased their contacts with the numerous groups drawn into the panchayat system, King Mahendra gradually reduced his personal involvement with issues and his personal contacts, which had enabled him to consistently outmaneuver his opposition.

Mahendra's ability to manipulate political and administrative institutions was greatly enhanced by the supportive relationship that had evolved between the king and the Royal Nepal Army. The Ranas' fall from power provided clear lessons about the importance of the military for the monarchy—Rana leaders' inability to modify the overcrowded facilities and their ambitious expectations for the overextended 25,000-man army that returned to Nepal after World War II led to factionalism and ultimately to the failure of the army to support the regime fully in battles with the Nepali Congress in 1950. King Tribhuvan, faced with widespread internal disorder, cut the army back to a more manageable size of 6,000 men and allowed a high-ranking Indian army team to radically restructure and retrain the army to improve its ability to control domestic disorder. More capable army leaders remained in command while their younger associates, generally from the same family background as the high Rana leadership, were sent to study in the military academies of Sandhurst and Dehra Dun.

From the beginning of his reign, Mahendra took an active interest in the army, frequently acting as his own minister of defense and shielding the army from the disruptive forces affecting the civilian bureaucracy. He gradually increased the strength of the army to 10,000 professional soldiers and saw that military budgets and privileges were expanded accordingly. After the army's key supportive role in the 1960 royal takeover, Mahendra even granted Tarai lands in excess of land-reform ceilings to a group of loyal military officers. At the same time, Mahendra gradually reduced the Indian influence in the army and kept active military officers strictly out of politics. Thus the army remained an important but isolated institution—technically oriented, conservative in outlook, and strongly supportive of the monarchy. If the monarchy should falter, the army could impose order. However, Mahendra's strategy has given young officers (whose interest in a more active role for the army in social and political matters may exceed that of the older generation on whom Mahendra relied) little experience in political leadership or civil administration. The army is unlikely to intrude as long as political processes remain orderly, but its shadow imposes considerable discipline on the strategies of political and administrative elites.

By the time Mahendra died in 1972, a broad range of new groups had been integrated into the complex of central institutions he had developed. The top secretaries, familiar with the demands of interest groups as well as with the state's development needs, were able to make some progress toward policy goals even while distributing state resources to maintain the support of new as well as established political groups. But the king's political strategy did not convince the illegal but still active party organizations to accept the panchayat system. Consequently, repressive police measures were still necessary to control party activity. State resources continued to be diverted to retain the loyalty of individual panchayat members, thereby contributing to the growing problem of corruption. Finally, Mahendra's disruptive method of controlling bureaucratic elites had not enabled the administration to build the organizational capability required for the extensive economic controls and sophisticated development projects undertaken by the government.

King Birendra's New Order

When King Birendra ascended the throne after the death of his father in January 1972, the monarchy's dominant position in politics was well established. The political instability that had forced Mahendra to rely on political accommodation was not a serious problem for Birendra. On the other hand, his father's inability to accelerate Nepal's development despite all his political controls had exposed the monarchy to the same charges of incompetence that Mahendra had leveled against the Nepali Congress regime. Furthermore, because of his extensive travels and foreign education, the young king was more familiar with the modern world and the international community's theories about economic development than he was with the intricacies of traditional Nepali court intrigues. He preferred interaction with his college-educated comrades to a policy of accommodation with Mahendra's old-style and often corrupt political allies. It was not surprising, then, that Mahendra's style of negotiation and intrigue was replaced by Birendra's emphasis on political discipline, efficient administration, and economic development. Mahendra's informal, ambiguous system of policy negotiations, which actively discouraged organizational development, gave way to Birendra's attempts to restructure the decision-making process within a formal, more stable institutional framework. Pledging to "unleash the mainspring of development," the new king set about reorganizing administrative and political institutions to make them more responsive to development demands.

Birendra chose to rely primarily on his palace secretariat (an organization that had provided little more than clerical support for Mahendra) to plan and control policies and institutional reorganizations. As crown prince, he had worked closely with a select group of young, educated administrators in the newly created Janch-Bujh Kendra (JBK—Research and Investigation Center) to plan policy and reorganizational strategies. When he became king, these same individuals assumed positions in the palace inner group and set about implementing their plans. The king met with new groups of educated administrators who were recruited for the policy-planning activities of the JBK, thus establishing contact with ambitious young elites and future leaders throughout the bureaucracy. However, Birendra spent less time than his father in private consultation with other important political elites. Hence, the palace secretariat became a powerful palace guard, limiting direct access to the king and forwarding requests only when deemed appropriate.

To gain firmer controls over their new policy initiatives,

the king and his palace advisers systematically weakened the policy negotiating position of the Central Secretariat. Mahendra's trusted secretaries were transferred or retired. The government-controlled press in Kathmandu condemned as improper the direct contacts between panchayat leaders and top administrative officials; several top administrators were charged with corruption and dismissed for their role in what had become the routine distribution of spoils. Secretaries in the ministries were not informed about policy deliberations at the JBK; at times, a secretary who under Mahendra would have been the primary author of a new policy would now simply be told to implement a palace/JBK-designed policy.

Birendra also introduced several reforms to improve administrative performance and reduce the ability of top administrators to alter or sabotage palace policies during implementation. Better record keeping and more objective measures to evaluate a department's policy activities were instituted, thereby improving the likelihood that intentional sabotage would be detected and the responsible officer punished. The National Planning Commission and Ministry of Finance developed a greater capability to review the progress made on development programs by the implementing agencies. Promotions within the administration were to be based on merit and service records, and the influence of top-level administrators over careers of junior officials was to be reduced, thereby orienting younger officials more toward formal policy requirements than toward the informal policy preferences of the secretaries and department chiefs. Furthermore, greater decision-making authority was to be delegated to field offices and the chief district officers, enabling them to handle the policy problems in their own areas and decreasing the need for local politicians to deal with central officials. Mahendra's strategy of continuous transfers among bureaucratic posts was rejected because of its disruptive effect on program implementation; instead, field officers were to serve for approximately thirty months in an assigned post before transfers would be allowed.

Although these reforms may in the future improve administrative stability and policy performance, their immediate effect was to destroy ongoing control mechanisms. The resultant administrative chaos demoralized the Central Secretariat and weakened its leadership in policy matters. Foreign-aid missions that had supported the central secretaries during Mahendra's reign were similarly excluded from the policy process; the more institutionalized interaction between donors and Birendra's Ministry of Finance required less secretarial intervention on behalf of each donor, while the availability of foreign-trained Nepali policy experts now obviated the need for all but the most specialized foreign advisers. Development funds provided by foreign-aid missions were needed more than ever, as were the administrative skills of the top secretaries. But both groups now found themselves reacting to palace initiatives rather than initiating and negotiating important policies. The reforms did not, however, prevent numerous private-interest groups with established bureaucratic contacts from channeling policy resources in directions they desired. Secretaries were now less willing and able to combat the influence of these groups, and the palace was unable to develop alternative sets of administrative controls refined enough to produce the implementation efforts desired by the palace. Thus palace attention shifted to the possibility of using political elites as a counterweight to bureaucratic influences on public policy.

Birendra and his advisers had allowed panchayat politics to continue with little direct guidance while administrative changes were introduced, but by 1974 the palace began a serious reevaluation of the panchayat system. Dissatisfaction with the system as it had evolved during Mahendra's reign was widespread, although the criticism varied with the critic's perspective. Development-oriented administrators at the center criticized the conservative bias of panchayat elites, who had been recruited primarily from traditional village elites and local notables. These administrators stressed the need both for the recruitment of new elites more favorably disposed toward the government's development programs and for administrative guidance of these inexperienced leaders. Political party sympathizers decried the unrepresentative character of elected panchayat officials and claimed that the system gave no democratic legitimacy whatsoever to the king's authoritarian regime. They demanded that the system be liberalized by introducing direct

national elections with the participation of organized parties
and guaranteed freedom of speech. Many established panchayat
elites, on the other hand, defended the indirect method of elections, which they could control more easily. They criticized the
arrogance of administrators who made policy decisions without
having to account for them publicly and called for a greater
devolution of authority to the elected panchayat institutions.

At first it appeared that Birendra favored some form of
liberalization. Party discipline, after all, would impose more
constraints on lower-level representatives than the panchayat
system had done. Although most party leaders had refused to
join the panchayat system and some continued their India-
based campaign of minor disruptions against the royal regime,
they posed a greater threat to the established panchayat elites
than they did to Birendra (at least as long as India supported
the regime). The king opened a dialogue with former party
leaders in Nepal, who for the most part had been ignored by
Mahendra after the panchayat system had been established.
Several of these leaders were appointed to a commission in
1974 to recommend changes in the panchayat system.

But the problem of preventing the emergence of a dominant
party that might again challenge the king's leadership apparently
remained unresolved, and the constitutional amendments
introduced in 1975 reconfirmed the partyless nature of the
panchayat system. The palace granted amnesty to some jailed
or exiled party members and encouraged them—as individuals—
to join the panchayat system. But Birendra also created a centrally controlled, hierarchical organization of loyal panchayat
elites to screen all candidates in panchayat elections. The palace
hoped that the Back-to-the-Village National Campaign (BVNC)
would be able to remove active party sympathizers from panchayat elections, recruit new panchayat elites loyal to Birendra
and supportive of his development programs, and discourage
ongoing corruption and sabotage of central policies by panchayat members. In operation, the BVNC usually approved only
one candidate in election contests, thereby eliminating all
electoral competition. But while the central committee was
appointed directly by the king and administered by one of his
advisers, the established panchayat elites, skilled as they are in

the intrigues of bureaucratically controlled elections, co-opted the BVNC and used it to protect their established positions against possible challenges from party members or from new palace recruits. The extent to which panchayat elites were more responsive to central-policy initiatives in return for greater security is difficult to ascertain, but no dramatic signs of change were evident.

Birendra's panchayat reforms were also designed to strengthen the local panchayat while dislodging some established leaders. Village panchayats were reorganized to reduce their number from the original 4,000 to the current 3,000 units, reducing thereby the trained personnel needed to provide capable local administration and intensifying competition for leadership within the larger unit. In the new panchayats, each of the nine wards elects five representatives to the panchayat assembly, which in turn elects the mayor and council and approves the village budget. Although direct election of the mayor—one of the more exciting electoral arenas in Mahendra's system—was eliminated, the expanded ward representation created official positions for a greater number of village elites from a potentially broader number of local groups. In support of this increased participation, a panchayat development tax reform authorized local panchayats to keep over half of the land taxes they collected for the panchayat budget while giving one-third to the central government and another 10 percent to the district panchayat. Introduced during the 1960s in several eastern Tarai panchayats, this tax increased significantly the number of small projects local panchayats could undertake. Administrative objections to the corruption, misuse, and ineptitude witnessed in the first panchayat undertakings slowed the expansion of this program during Mahendra's reign, but the present government began expanding the program again to encourage local political involvement in the national development effort.

Minor changes at other panchayat levels demonstrated the king's ambivalence toward increasing effective (rather than symbolic) political participation in central policy processes. The Graduates' Constituency (whose representatives had been among the most troublesome for the government) and the class organizations no longer elected representatives to the National Panchayat. The zonal assembly was abolished and a larger district-wide electorate for National Panchayat elections proposed, but the predilection of the BVNC to appoint panchayat members made such electoral changes rather insignificant. Disputes between BVNC committee members and panchayat members weakened the position of both in relation to administrative officers, particularly at the central and district levels. Furthermore, Birendra tended to choose more cabinet members from the ranks of administrative technocrats rather than from elected panchayat members. Thus the cabinet became even less answerable to the National Panchayat, particularly after the BVNC assumed the function of insuring that National Panchayat members support important palace initiatives. Although political elites participated in central policy processes as individual cabinet members, Birendra was not able to devise an institutional basis for their participation that would associate them more closely with the panchayat system without reducing their responsiveness to the palace's policy initiatives.

By the late 1970s, the administrative and political reforms introduced by Birendra had produced a highly centralized policymaking system in which expert analysis, not political compromise, had become the dominant mode of decision making. Policy issues that interested the palace were assigned to ad hoc JBK study groups, which were closely supervised by a palace secretary. The resultant reports served as the basis for discussion within the palace secretariat and among carefully chosen outside participants. Administrators might be consulted about particular issues but often were not involved until after the palace secretariat had made its recommendations and the king had endorsed the policy. Cabinet and National Panchayat approval was required before the bill became law, but if members had not already persuaded the palace secretaries to make desired changes during informal discussions, they had little chance of influencing the bill during the process of formal approval.

The numerous ethnic, regional, partisan, familial, and other political groups mobilized first by the political parties and then by the panchayat system are today not easily excluded from access to state resources. Groups excluded from the institutions that formulate policies try to influence the implementation of central policies at any level of administration where they can be effective. Political networks (including traditional as well as new groups mobilized by the parties and the panchayat system) maneuver skillfully within the panchayat and administrative institutions to maintain their claims on state resources; however, one would suspect they gain little sense of identification with the political system. Participation is a negative process, achieved through sabotaging central policies and capturing state resources for personal use. Thus the present system runs the risk of satisfying few, if any, of the political actors; central policies remain unimplemented and political groups are frustrated with the state's lack of response to their problems.

The monarchy continues to be the axis around which the political life of Nepal revolves, but political legitimacy depends on the charisma of the crown, not on the elaborate and basically unrepresentative system of governmental institutions. Yet Nepalis of many diverse political persuasions who perceive the throne as, on balance, a positive force in economic development and in the preservation of Nepal's national identity must be concerned with the fate of monarchical regimes and their institutions in other nations. The most obvious lesson from recent developments in Iran, Ethiopia, and Afghanistan is that an unwillingness to share power in *real* terms leads eventually to a total loss of power. Nepal's unexpected political crisis in the spring of 1979 brought the lesson closer to home: a massive (for Nepal) student movement in April and May accompanied by sporadic but at times violent protest movements in many parts of the country—some inspired by local issues—presented the royal regime with a situation that was not easily controlled. First the minister of education and then the entire cabinet were forced to resign. Finally, on May 24, King Birendra announced that a national referendum would be held based on adult franchise in which the people of Nepal could choose between the panchayat system or a multiparty system of government (presumably under the leadership of the monarch).

Two points should be clear: good intentions are not

enough, and charismatic appeals can only provide an uncertain basis of support. Even early in his reign, King Birendra comprehended the dilemma he faced and sought to project a new and vital image of the monarchy. In the process, however, he accepted the advice proffered by both Nepali and foreign advisers to give the highest priority to economic development and to allow the political system to rest in cold storage. In other words, they were advising him to emulate the Shah of Iran.

Despite the deficiencies in the regime's central controls, which have become obvious to all, the concept that sharing power can expand rather than diminish power at the center was not persuasive to the king's advisers. Yet central institutions that would increase participation and the sharing of power—disruptive though they may be of well-formulated but unrealized palace policies—may be necessary to improve the implementation of development policies and increase the royal regime's ability to survive the inevitable challenges from its changing domestic and international environments. Stable, more substantial roles in important policy processes would enable political and administrative leaders to identify with the regime as well as with its major policy initiatives. Furthermore, institutions that involve more groups in policymaking could establish broad policy coalitions while objectives were being formulated. Although the ensuing policies would inevitably reflect analytically unappealing compromises, coalitions with vested interest in policy could intervene to help solve unavoidable implementation problems.

King Birendra has at times shown an interest in liberalizing his regime, but the division within the "palace guard" between hard-liners and moderates—particularly on the issue of political parties—has blocked proposed liberal reforms. Reconciliation between the palace and political-party leaders jailed or exiled after Mahendra's takeover in 1960 remains elusive. As the only organized and vocal opposition to the regime, the party leaders have even gained a measure of sympathy from bureaucratic and panchayat sources frustrated with their reassignment to nominal roles in the present system.

The parties, however, are divided on organizational and

ideological issues, which are often superimposed on personality clashes that go back to the 1950s. Only two party movements, the Nepali Congress and the Communists, have been able to maintain an organizational structure in a number of areas of the country through two decades of formal illegality, but even they are divided into several factions with different policy and political perspectives. The Nepali Congress consists of three ill-defined groups: a moderate faction largely associated with two ministers of the 1959–1960 ministry, S. P. Upadhyaya and Subarna Shamsher (now deceased); an "extremist" group in which Ganeshman Singh and K. P. Bhattarai ahve been the principal spokesmen; and a centrist group in which B. P. Koirala has usually been the dominant personality. Numerous sub-groups have also emerged over the years, mostly led by local leaders with unclear ties to the national leadership. But this factionalism within the Nepali Congress would appear to be largely superficial, and it is likely that the different groups are capable of effective cooperation when necessary. The divisions among the Communists may prove to be a greater problem, because the two main factions of the party are financed by the implacably hostile Soviet and Chinese embassies in Kathmandu. A unified Communist party would be difficult to achieve and would probably not endure for long. There are numerous other "parties" in Nepal, representing the minor political parties in the pre-1960 system, but they all lack any real organization or visible support base. An extreme leftist faction, for instance, collaborated with conservative, pro-panchayat forces in opposing the referendum, presumably because both would be isolated in a multiparty electoral system.[1]

The royal announcement on May 24, 1979, of the forthcoming national referendum on a political system was welcomed enthusiastically by party leaders, indicating that a reconciliation between King Birendra and the political parties might be close at hand. But the interplay of forces within the palace added considerable uncertainty because conflicts between panchayat and party elites could still be used to deny both groups a more substantial role in important policy processes. The king's determination to introduce basic political reforms, however, is widely acknowledged, even among oppositionist elements. In his Constitution Day announcement of December 16, 1979,

King Birendra declared that regardless of the referendum's outcome, the prime minister will be selected by and responsible to a new National Legislature elected on the basis of adult suffrage. Such reforms are essential for the development of the nation, the stability of the political system, and, ultimately, the survival of Nepal as an independent country.

Notes

1. Such unusual alignments have occurred in the past as well. The BVNC, for instance, recruited a number of so-called "Naxalite" Communists in its district-level campaigns against both the established local panchayat elites and the workers of the more moderate Nepali Communist and Congress organizations.

3

The Emergent
National Society

Nepal is a nation of villages. More than 96 percent of its 14 million inhabitants (1980 estimates) live in small rural settlements with an average of fewer than 600 residents. The urban population has increased somewhat more rapidly than the national average annual increase of 2.2 percent during the last decade, but most of the migration caused by growing population pressure on limited cultivable lands in the hills has been to less densely settled areas of the Tarai rather than to the towns. Because of internal migration, the population of several hill districts has increased only 1 percent annually, while some Tarai districts have grown by more than 5 percent. Yet these major demographic shifts of the recent decades have not changed the predominantly rural character of Nepali society.

As in most peasant societies, family and kinship relations form the most important social networks for villagers. Traditionally, several generations of the extended family lived together in the same household and jointly farmed the family lands, which were divided among the sons only after the death of the father. Marriages were arranged by the families, and the wife generally became a part of the husband's household, sometimes moving far away from her native village. The modern trend, which has long been a practice for some ethnic groups, is for a married son to establish a separate household when the first child is born and to farm individually his share of the father's land.

The average household in modern Nepal has five to six members, although family size varies considerably due in part to the uncertainties of child rearing. The average married woman gives birth to 7 children if she lives to be fifty years old, but Nepal's infant mortality rate of 175 to 200 deaths per 1,000 births—among the highest in Asia—reduces family size. Life expectancy at birth is only forty years, although individuals who survive childhood will on the average live to be sixty. As the crude annual death rate, which is presently between 20 and 25 people per 1,000, continues to decline, one would expect women to bear fewer children to keep family size approximately the same. But even if women give birth to fewer children, the annual birthrate of about 42 children per 1,000 will probably continue because of the age distribution of the population— more than 40 percent of the population is under the age of fifteen years, which means that the number of women reaching childbearing age will be increasing in the near future.

Within the family, men traditionally do the agricultural work while women raise the children and manage the household tasks. However, during the planting and harvest seasons when labor is in short supply, women work long hours in the fields as well. And in areas with a chronic labor shortage, particularly in hill villages where a large percentage of the male population serves in the Gurkha units of the British and Indian armies, it is not uncommon for women to farm the fields alone. Both men and women practice various household crafts, particularly in more isolated areas. Even the children are kept busy watching their younger brothers and sisters, helping with household tasks, and tending the family's livestock. Schooling suffers because of these household chores, especially where the girls are concerned—only 1 percent of Nepal's female population receives a formal education, compared to 6 percent of the male. Literacy rates are considerably higher, due to the prevalence of informal tutoring, but show the same discrepancy between men (25 percent literacy) and women (5 percent literacy). With the growth of village schools since 1950 the difference in education between men and women has become more pronounced; 15 percent of the male population between the ages of twenty and twenty-four has had some schooling compared to less than 2 percent of the female population.

The simplified picture of the typical Nepali family given

above and the aggregate demographic statistics do not, of course, do justice to the broad range of Nepali life-styles. To understand the different patterns of family life and the social interactions beyond the immediate family, it is necessary to know the ethnic identities of Nepali groups as well as the status hierarchy that evolved during the Rana era and the recent egalitarian trends in Nepal's emergent national society.

Ethnic Identity and Its Origin

The ethnic identity of most Nepali citizens is readily apparent to their countrymen by their dress, language, habits, and facial features and frequently determines the kind of preliminary interaction that takes place when strangers meet. When asked about their identity by an outsider, they would normally respond with the name of their ethnic group, since ethnic identity is one of the major factors that limits one's choice of a marriage partner, friends, and career opportunities. Indeed, the readily identifiable ethnic groups offer an important and deceptively simple perspective for viewing Nepal's complex social milieu.

Social scientists have had considerable difficulty distinguishing specific characteristics that can consistently classify Nepalis into the groups with which they self-identify. As a first approximation, one can divide groups into two rough categories: (1) those who speak Tibeto-Burman languages, have "Mongolian" facial features, live at higher altitudes and in the northern parts of the country, and observe religious beliefs considerably influenced by Buddhism; and (2) those who speak Sanskrit-derived languages, have Indoaryan features, live at lower elevations and in southern regions, and practice Hindu religious customs.

The Tibeto-Burman groups are believed to have migrated at various times from the east or from Tibet. These groups account for perhaps 45 percent of Nepal's population, and each group composes a majority in its traditional areas. The Newars, the earliest known arrivals and most accomplished artisans and merchants in Nepal, are centered primarily in the Kathmandu valley, but they have also established trade towns throughout the central hills in pursuit of their commercial interests. The

Limbus in the far eastern and the Rais in the middle eastern hills, two of the more autonomous hill groups, are probably descendants of the Kiranti tribes mentioned in ancient Indian texts. The Tamangs in the central hills (numerically the largest of these ethnic groups), the Gurungs to the west, and Magars to their southwest arrived before the major migrations from the plains. The Sherpas and other northernmost groups are presumably the latest arrivals, with languages and customs still very similar to their Tibetan neighbors to the north.

The most important of the Indoaryan groups are the hill Brahmans and Chetris (Kshatriya/warriors in the Hindu hierarchy), who dominate the major political institutions and have settled throughout the rice-growing elevations in the hills, where they are frequently counted among the local elites. Their language, Nepali, has become the national language and the common language for communication among most groups in the country. Perhaps a dozen small, untouchable occupational caste groups like cobblers (Sarki) and tailors (Damai) are scattered in various places in the hills, but the complex caste system as it exists in India appears only in Nepal's southern Tarai area. The plains people (Madheshis) who inhabit this border area comprise almost 25 percent of Nepal's population. In addition to numerous local groupings in the caste hierarchy, plains peoples are divided into three Hindi-related language groups that, unlike the hill groups, share literary and cultural traditions with a large percentage of the population in the adjacent Indian border states. These Tarai language groups are Maithili in the east, Bhojpuri in the center, and Awadhi in the west.

The simplified twofold division of ethnic groups breaks down on closer examination. Most groups in the hills have adopted many Hindu practices, which have taken their place alongside Buddhist and shamanistic practices. In fact, it is not uncommon to find elements of Buddhism and Hinduism combined in the numerous religious festivals celebrated throughout Nepal. The pantheon of deities worshipped by a single Nepali family frequently includes deities from both of these religions as well as from other local religious traditions. Families do not perceive these religious traditions to be in conflict with each other or with other more recent "scientific" beliefs; the same family may call in a priest for some problems, a shaman for others, and a doctor trained in Western medicine for yet other kinds of problems. The cultural boundaries between Hinduism and Buddhism, consequently, are not well demarcated in Nepal.

Furthermore, the variation between subgroups within broader ethnic groupings is great. The Hindu practices of hill Brahmans are based on ancient Hindu texts with certain concessions to religious practices of other hill groups. Thus they are quite distinct from the practices of the Tarai Brahmans, which have been influenced by modern Hindu reform movements and secular trends in India. Even within the ranks of hill Brahmans, the rivalry between Kumai and Purbia subgroups has led to considerable internal conflict. After many centuries of rule by Hindu kings, the Newars in the Kathmandu valley have both Buddhist and Hindu subgroups; the variety of characteristics found within these subgroups makes it difficult to classify the Newars in the Tibeto-Burman ethnic family. Similarly, many groups are composed of regional subgroups who speak mutually unintelligible dialects (if, in fact, they speak the same language at all) and some subgroups who speak only Nepali. Ethnic identities like the Tamang may indeed have been imposed on small groups that had few common characteristics. Several Tarai groups—the Rajbansis, Gangais, and others in the east, as well as the Tharus from east to west—have physical features resembling Tibeto-Burman groups but speak Sanskrit-derived languages. And the Muslim groups comprising almost 10 percent of the plains people have remained as segregated from the dominant Hindu plains groups in Nepal as they have in India.

The inconsistencies involved in identifying ethnic characteristics are not surprising, however, since ethnic identity in modern Nepal is primarily the product of long interaction among numerous ethnic groups as conditioned by the dominant Hindu culture. The process of Sanskritization described in Chapter 1 affected more than just the tribal elites absorbed into the flexible Chetri group and the Brahman priests who sanctioned this absorption. For within each present-day ethnic grouping (jat), there are several lineage or clan subgroups (thar) that vary in status, in part according to the degree to which they celebrate Hindu ceremonies, accept Brahmanic ritual

taboos, and speak the national language. Particularly since unification in the late eighteenth century, ambitious leaders of
local clans have abstained publicly from alcohol and unclean
food and have recruited Brahmans to perform family ceremonies
and trace ancestry to possible high-caste origins. Established
Hindu credentials would enable the family to intermingle (and
perhaps, over many generations, to intermarry) with other local
notables and the representatives of the Hindu state. By ele-
vating the status of his clan, the leader not only gains access to
state powers and potentially lucrative administrative contacts
but also secures the clan's prominent position within its region
and ethnic community.

During the last two centuries, Brahmans and Chetris,
Nepal's most aggressive colonists, enjoyed an advantage over
other hill groups in competing for state favors because of their
cultural affinity with the increasingly powerful district officers.
Indeed, the symbiotic relationship between central Chetri elites
and the local Brahmans and Chetris situated throughout the
country may explain why other ethnic elites from the preunifi-
cation principalities never made the transition to Kathmandu
after unification. In any case, wherever local ethnic identities
obscured the political loyalty of elites, the central government
or district officer could encourage new Brahman or Chetri
settlements, strengthen their existing leadership, and eventually
play them off against the non-Hindu ethnic elites.

Hill Brahmans and Chetris never penetrated deeply into
Tarai society, which partially accounts for the failure to integrate
the Tarai into Nepal's social order. They were discouraged
from clearing and settling jungle areas in the Tarai's hot malarial
climate, so different from the moderate climate of their homes
in the hills. But more importantly they had to compete with an
already Sanskritized Hindu social hierarchy that had its own
Brahmans and Kshatriya groups and established relationships
with major cultural and language groups. Thus, because of their
government contacts, hill Brahmans and Chetris became absentee
overlords and revenue contractors, but rarely established members of the sophisticated Tarai society.

In the hills, however, Brahmans and Chetris invariably
went beyond the immediate needs of central officials in pene-

trating the spheres of influence of other ethnic communities. Ethnic identity, consequently, was revived as a defensive weapon used by established elites in ethnic communities to prevent encroachment by these or other groups seeking land and influence in the area. Thus to elevate their clan in the Hindu hierarchy recognized by the state, non-Hindu ethnic elites had to use great subtlety to avoid undercutting ethnic traditions that excluded outsiders from their villages, lest those traditions be turned against them by competing village elites.

The central government, particularly under the Rana regime, tended to encourage ethnic elites in their quest for higher status within their own group. Whereas the earlier legal code of King Ram Shah of Gorkha prescribed social regulation only for the higher-caste Hindus, the 1854 legal code introduced by the first Rana prime minister included detailed provisions regulating relationships within and among the major ethnic groups in Nepal. Although these regulations dealt primarily with the rights and duties of Brahmans and Chetris, they also recognized the legal identity of other groups, assured the continued ethnic identity of these groups by forbidding intermarriage, and based their legal responsibilities on their particular customary practices. Furthermore, the codes officially recognized the higher status of the more Hinduized clans within each group, thereby enhancing their monopoly on state contacts within the group. And finally, Rana administrative reforms generally preserved local controls over land and local trade monopolies, enabling the established ethnic elites to prevent encroachment by other groups. To some degree the Ranas were simply forced to accept the de facto controls these ethnic elites possessed in many rural areas, but elites who were willing to identify with the Hindu principles of the regime were certainly preferred by Kathmandu to those who opposed Hinduism and all forms of state intervention. Besides, the less politically knowledgeable ethnic elites served as a useful counterbalance to powerful rural Brahman or Chetri notables who might, through alliance with the central political opposition, pose a greater threat to the regime.

Thus, the ethnic pattern that had emerged by the end of the Rana era in 1950 featured ethnically pure villages led by state-confirmed Sanskritized ethnic leaders with high status in their communities. Notables with established bases in Brahman and Chetri settlements vied with notables from locally dominant non-Hindu ethnic groups for district-level status and influence. High-ranking bureaucrats were from Kathmandu-based Brahman, Chetri, and Newar families, who also recruited rural elites for district office staffs. Even today, of all rural elites, only the sons of Brahman, Chetri, and Newar notables have been at all successful at making inroads into the Kathmandu elites' monopoly on bureaucratic positions. Brahmans enjoyed the highest caste status throughout the country, but the high-ranking Chetris, and particularly the Ranas, enjoyed the most powerful and prestigious positions in the central social milieu.

Persisting Traditions of Land and Authority Relationships

The pattern of ethnic interactions alone cannot account for many seemingly contradictory relationships in modern Nepali society. Why, for example, does a Brahman tenant (supposedly of the highest status in the Hindu caste hierarchy) kowtow to his lower-status Limbu landlord, who, in turn, responds to the personal wishes of a Newar district officer? To understand the wider range of social intercourse and conflict, it is also necessary to be aware of common patterns of authority relationships. Although less readily identifiable than ethnic interactions, these relationships illuminate more clearly the hierarchy of status levels linking village society with the national social milieu.

The heterogeneity of authority relationships posed as great a problem for the Shah dynasty's attempts to integrate and administer its conquered territories as did the variety of ethnic identities. Not surprisingly, the ancient Shastras and the Code of Manu (Manusmriti), which provided the basis for the legal code's prescription of rigidly separate and hierarchical relations among ethnic groups, have influenced the state's prescription for hierarchical authority relationships between individual status levels as well—between the patriarch and his extended family, between the landlord and his tenants, the tax contractor and

the landholders in his district, the administrator and his sub-
ordinates, or the political leader and his administrative supporters. The specific duties and privileges involved in these relationships vary considerably in different social settings. Yet
they all share a common pattern: a personal relationship is
defined between the higher-status "patron," who controls the
means of livelihood (generally land or the authority to appoint
an officer of state), and the lower-status "client," who needs
this livelihood. The client, in addition to various acts of personal
loyalty that demonstrate his acceptance of the patron's higher
status, performs services required by the patron (cultivation of
land, aid to the patron's political conspiracies), creating a mutual
dependence despite the unequal status and command of resources. Both patron and client are bound by community and
legal traditions, yet both seek to change these traditions in
response to new or unusual circumstances: patrons command
that personal loyalty or new services should be given beyond
traditional strictures, while clients lay claim to a portion of the
patron's "right" to control the means of livelihood.

State authority and central laws become the final arbiter
of social relations when disputes are appealed beyond the immediate relationship. Such appeals frequently occur when ambitious patrons attempt to annex the rights and clients of a
neighboring patron, when new clients compete for favorable
treatment by a patron whose resources have already been committed to other clients, or when changes in accepted values
challenge previous rights and obligations. Thus, any patron
vulnerable to such challenges will seek the protection of an even
higher-status patron who can defend his interests when the need
arises, extending the chain of patron-client ties to the highest
arenas of political power. When a small group dominates the
central institutions of a well-integrated patrimonial state and no
centralized religious, economic, or other cultural institutions
provide a competing source of social arbitration, the social
order can be visualized as a giant pyramid made up of layers of
patron-client clusters, with the patrons of the lower clusters
forming the clientele for the less numerous patrons in the layer
above. During the century of Rana rule, Nepal's society was
slowly evolving toward just such an order.

Vertical Ties in Rural Society

Authority relationships under the Rana regime depended primarily on control of land. An ascending chain of vertical relationships linked tenants at the lowest level to landlords, then to village elites, to local notables, and finally to district officers of the central government. Since by the end of the Rana era more than 60 percent of Nepal's cultivated land was controlled by landlords, the various relationships that developed between landlord and tenant in different areas were not only important in their own right but also indicative of trends throughout the society. At one extreme, a tenant, through enslavement (officially illegal since 1926) or debt bondage, was completely dependent on the will of the landlord. He lived in the landlord's compound and acted as a household servant as well as an agricultural laborer. At the other extreme, a relatively higher status tenant owned his home and perhaps some land and independently cultivated the plot of land he rented. The most independent tenants paid only a specified amount of rent, but normally the landlord would take a percentage of the harvest (frequently half directly from the threshing floor in addition to collecting food loans and interest charges, seed for the next year, and other miscellaneous charges). Local traditions defined a range of tenancy conditions between these extremes.

Tenancy relationships and the consequent status system varied from settlement to settlement, a fact that has complicated the government's efforts to reform tenancy conditions. One entire village of tenants, whose makeshift huts surround the landlord's large stucco house, might be completely subservient to the landlord, while a neighboring village with more dispersed landownership might have a more graduated social ranking in which some assertive tenant families were actually better off than the poorer landowners. In general, however, tenancy traditions were consistent within large geographic areas for villages having similar patterns of agricultural cycles, migration and settlement histories, and population densities. In hill areas, where ownership was generally more dispersed and tenancy status less onerous, these traditions favored fixed rents, particularly on nonirrigated lands. In the Tarai, where ownership was frequently much more concentrated, most tenants paid a percentage of the harvest. Bondage and service obligations were also more common in the Tarai, particularly in the areas settled during the twentieth century under the supervision of agricultural contractors. These wealthy entrepreneurs preferred to recruit low-status tribal groups (Tharus, Rajbansis, Sattars) who lacked the power to demand ownership rights and thus would leave the contractors in full legal possession of the land. Intermediate tenancy positions also developed in such areas because the contractor needed subcontractors to settle and pay taxes on smaller plots. All landlords (with the exception of the small group of privileged birta landowners who lived primarily in Kathmandu) possessed their land only insofar as they performed certain obligations required by the state. Thus the state agent who controlled land records and saw that these obligations were fulfilled occupied a status position one rung higher than the village landholder, whether landlord or owner-cultivator. As with landlord-tenant relationships, the interaction between village agents (who were frequently recruited locally) and villagers varied throughout Nepal, particularly since the agents' official powers varied with the land-tenure classification—i.e., raiker, birta, jagir, kipat, or guthi—of the village.[1]

In all these tenure systems, the village agent of necessity lived in the village and knew its residents intimately. Generally, agents would be recruited locally from the same ethnic group as the village's landholders. Villagers who increased their family wealth through shrewd moneylending or intensive agricultural activities vied for this position, which generally insured them a high local status level and provided a basis for activities beyond village boundaries. Upward mobility was limited, of course, since only members of the Sanskritized clans officially recognized by the state were likely to be appointed. Besides, the village agent's local powers were so substantial and his knowledge of village land and tax records so important to the government and other villagers that he was seldom replaced. Not infrequently, the agent's son would be appointed when his father died. Yet the agent was vulnerable if village tax assessments were raised, if villagers (particularly from opposing factions) delayed or refused to pay taxes, or if no tax relief was granted in times of

poor harvests. In these situations the agent required support
from local notables of the next higher-status group, whose
influence and primary arena of social interaction extended well
beyond the village boundary.

Local notables occupied positions in the official hierarchy
between village agents and district administrators (or privileged
landowners, who employed them to oversee private village
agents). Revenue villages were generally organized into larger
areas supervised by tax contractors, who in turn were responsible
to the district revenue office. In order to qualify for these potentially lucrative but sometimes disastrous contractual positions,
a notable had to possess considerable land, frequently scattered
in various villages. This land was pledged as a security bond in
the event he failed to collect the revenue specified in the contract. Many local notables were undoubtedly the descendants
of Bharadars from the principalities of the pre-1770 era, since
only notables with extensive informal controls over village
agents and other clients throughout their area of operation
would be able to meet long-term contractual obligations even
after bad harvests. But traditional elite families had to compete
successfully for land and customs revenue collection contracts,
trade monopolies, and land reclamation grants in order to preserve their wealth, official authority, and government contacts. Since ambitious village elites vied to outbid established
notables for such contracts, competition was at times quite
intense. If successfully exploited, these contracts would enable
a village elite to expand his family's operations far enough
beyond the confines of the village to obtain the status of a local
notable. And notables from neighboring areas and administrative centers, particularly Brahmans and Chetris, would attempt
to replace existing contractors through a strategy of ethnic politics and bureaucratic intrigues. As a consequence, local notables
required relatively secure relations with the bureaucracy in
order to maintain their status position.

Bureaucratic and Political Patrons

The two most striking social changes during the Rana era
were the consolidation of a landed aristocracy (the Ranas)
that monopolized all important political offices and top social

ranks, and the elevation of a Kathmandu-based bureaucratic elite to a political and social rank superior to the formerly dominant local notables. During the Rana's long period of relatively stable rule, reforms were patiently but persistently implemented through the bureaucracy to reshape existing relationships among local notables, village elites, landholders, and cultivators into a more uniform system consistent with the needs and purposes of the emerging aristocracy. As a result, the number of central offices multiplied and clerical staffs at both central and district offices expanded to control numerous functions and to record transactions previously left to the discretion of local notables or village agents.

The Rana bureaucracy developed out of the traditional familial alliance system (chakari). All major government offices were controlled by Ranas and were located in the officers' residences, where the officers' client families would perform the needed administrative and clerical work. As an office's functions grew more complex, a bureaucratic corps developed, an experienced staff that did not follow the Rana officer when he succeeded to a higher office. An intricate system of chakari evolved—still influential today—in which the bureaucrat's survival depended on his ability to retain the loyalty of his original patron family and to establish a favorable relationship with his new superior by giving small gifts, attending his informal court, judiciously flattering his views, and performing small favors to demonstrate loyalty and submission. As a result of this system, Kathmandu families with established contacts, clerical skills, and experience in bureaucratic infighting (primarily the elite Brahman and Newar families who were politically less threatening to the Ranas than other Chetri families) were able to dominate all levels of the central bureaucracy below the Rana officers.

As the bureaucracy expanded and became more powerful, so did the practice of chakari. Lower-level bureaucrats established chakari relationships with older bureaucratic elites in higher positions. In district offices, where lower-ranking Ranas or bureaucratic officials not connected with the area were sent to "rule" for five-to-ten-year periods, local notables requiring a bureaucratic service were generally expected to present some sort of token tribute to acknowledge the officer's status superiority and establish a personal basis for the required transaction. When expansion of district-office functions increased the need for clerical staff, local notables competed through chakari relationships to place their sons in such positions. Even though staff members made no important decisions, their knowledge of bureaucratic routines, their access to information, and their possible influence over the district officer were important in securing new grants or contracts and in protecting existing grants from the conspiracies of other notables or village elites. But local staff members were seldom promoted to bureaucratic offices in Kathmandu.

By 1950, the system of state authority reflected, in its legal framework if not always in actuality, a relatively clear national status hierarchy. The Ranas, with their monopoly on military rank and social prestige, their privileged landowner status and palatial residences, and their observance of prescribed Hindu rituals and carefully arranged marriages (especially with the royal family and reputable princely families in India), dominated Nepal socially as well as politically. The Kathmandu-based bureaucratic elites filled the secondary ranks and inter-mingled with deposed political elites from the pre-Rana era who managed to retain some wealth and social status despite the Rana monopoly. In the countryside, the local notables and village agents who performed necessary tasks for the central regime gained prestige and power from their recognized position with the central regime, thus supplementing their authority based on local traditions.

This hierarchy was not, of course, a well-defined pyramidal order in which each level was linked exclusively with the next level. Some local notables, particularly in the western hills, enjoyed direct contacts with Rana and other central elites and thus higher status than some district officers. Other local notables with well-established support bases refused to be subservient to the bureaucrats, who, after all, needed their cooperation to collect government revenues and preserve law and order. Astute district officers sought direct relations with village agents to weaken the influence of such local notables, and the central government forbade tax contractors to appoint relatives as village elites. Similarly, the court system had gradually introduced property rights that limited the landholder's dependence on village agents. And ethnic identities, of course, complicated the local status order that arose from competition among the various groups to improve their status position within the continuously evolving national social order.

Democratic Reforms and the Emergent Panchayat Social Order

The new political leadership that assumed power in 1951 introduced various forms of democratic legislation that altered the legal basis of landownership and ethnic interaction, abolished privileged social positions (except in the case of the royal family), and restructured authoritative relationships. Intent on undermining certain aspects of the Rana social order, the new leaders encouraged modernizing influences that the previous leadership had kept to a minimum. Hierarchical relationships that had formed the basis of Rana legal codes had already been eroded by several forces: increased market-oriented economic activities and expanded trade with India; the disappearance in the hill areas of reclaimable wastelands between settlements; the establishment of relatively independent courts to defend property rights against the whims of the bureaucrats and aristocrats; the return of thousands of Gurkha soldiers who had been exposed to new ideas and cultures during World War II; and the education of a new generation of Nepali notables, bureaucrats, and aristocrats in Indian schools, where egalitarian ideals of social and political justice had gained prominence during the long campaign for India's political independence.

The Rana regime was not a victim of rebellion by lower social echelons against their "feudal leaders" (as popular rhetoric has claimed at times). Intellectual foment from the dramatic changes taking place in India did, however, inspire an opposition movement in Nepal that used democratic ideals to attack the increasingly divided Rana aristocracy and undermine the legitimacy of the social order it represented. In the new political order, competition among various groups of notables, aristocrats, and bureaucratic elites sharpened the egalitarian ideology into a political weapon: bureaucrats favored land reforms that would weaken the social controls of the aristocrats and notables, who in turn battled each other to claim the legitimate democratic leadership over the bureaucracy.

Legal changes in landlord-tenant relationships, enacted after a decade of debate in the 1964 Land Reform Act, provide a clear example of legislative attempts to replace hierarchical patron-client interactions with standardized contractual relationships between, in legal concepts, social equals. The 1963 legal code had already abolished various unpaid labor obligations, thereby diminishing the superior status of the landlord or tax agent. In the 1964 act, the tenant was granted an inalienable right (except in very limited circumstances) to the land he was cultivating as long as he paid the amount of rent prescribed by the state. Furthermore, personal debt bondage was eliminated by transferring tenants' debts to a "ward committee," a credit institution designed in part to eliminate the potentially exploitative relationship between moneylender and debtor. In short, tenants gained a legal landholding right that, despite the greater wealth of the landlord, established a contractual relationship with no implied status inferiority.

Reforms also attacked other land controls that had provided the legal basis of the Rana order. Most of the aristocracy's privileged birta and jagir lands were converted to common raiker tenure and distributed to tenants (often not the actual cultivators) registered on the lands, thus depriving the predominantly Rana birta holders of their authority over the villages, their prestige as landowners, and, except for small amounts of compensation, their traditional source of income. (By this time, the wealthiest families had invested much of their landed income in Indian economic ventures.) Local notables and village agents lost their claim to represent state authority when the system of tax contracting was abolished—land revenue was to be collected by the bureaucracy, and the administrative and judicial functions previously performed by local notables and village agents were assigned to the new panchayat institutions. The large landholdings that had provided a stable basis for the power and prestige of local notables were to be broken up by prescribing limits on individual landownership. Although some notables retained control over their lands and tenants through arrangements of questionable legality, the prestige formerly assured by the possession of large landholdings was now replaced by disparagement. Such notables were viewed as "feudal elements" or "exploiters," especially in the eyes of the middle-level landowners whose status was most elevated by these reforms. By attacking the concentrations of individual wealth and authority, the new egalitarian legal principles sought to establish relatively equal status as well as uniform duties and obligations among all landowners.

Democratic legislation did not, of course, immediately alter the Rana social order, but it did provide a new ideological basis for the social hierarchy and strengthen the client's bargaining position vis-à-vis his patron. Only a few tenants in an area needed to assert their rights when government officials arrived to redefine the landlord-tenant relationship throughout the village. In the more economically advanced and politically sophisticated areas, tenants who were registered were no longer subservient to their landlords. In other areas, however, many tenants were illegally evicted and landholders reduced to tenancy during the process of redefinition, the ironic victims of egalitarian social policies. And in yet other areas, particularly in the hills, tenancy practices have been little affected by the land-reform laws. Similarly, many village elites and local notables adversely affected by changes in the tax system (which still have not been introduced in all areas) successfully reestablished their claim to state authority within the panchayat system. But even for those who made the transition, the influence and prestige they acquire as panchayat "representatives" fall far short of the fear and awe they commanded in the Rana order.

The legal basis for interaction among ethnic groups was also radically changed by Kathmandu-based reformers. The 1963 legal code deleted previous regulations enforcing both the segregation of ethnic groups and untouchability. Guarantees entitling every citizen to equal treatment before the law replaced the special status granted to higher castes in previous codes. Indirect effects of other legislation also weakened the ability of ethnic elites to enforce ethnic traditions. Land reform eliminated the village agents' informal power to enforce traditional bans against selling village land to outside ethnic groups.

Similarly, when the agent's judicial powers were delegated to the panchayat (which generally contains several villages of different ethnic groups), ethnic elites encountered difficulty in imposing their group's customary social regulations on villagers in the name of the state.

But democratic reforms affecting religious practices and ethnic identity were not immediately and strictly enforced. When untouchables tried to assert the rights guaranteed in the 1963 legal code by entering the most important Hindu temple in Kathmandu, for example, the government argued that such intrusions impinged on the rights of others to worship according to their tradition and would not support them. Compliance with such reforms has depended on gradual adjustments in the ongoing processes of social change. In the tolerant boom towns and new settlement areas, such adjustments have already encouraged fraternizing among ethnic groups—for instance, intercaste marriages not tolerated in most older villages are accepted. Yet the process of Sanskritization goes on despite the change in legal codes. Greater legal tolerance for ethnic interaction, combined with the growing intrusion of government institutions into village life, may in fact have encouraged a greater number of rural ethnic groups and clans to adopt Hindu customs and seek other necessary social credentials (i.e., education) in order to gain acceptance (and protection) in the expanding circles of elite discourse. Such unforeseeable ramifications of induced social change (particularly when complex phenomena like ethnic identities are involved) support the wisdom of a long-term enforcement strategy that relies on gradual adjustments in social institutions steadily directed toward the desired goal.

To replace the land-based vertical linkages that integrated the Rana social order, the state established local, district, and national panchayat institutions, which, by creating new arenas of conflict, have the potential to become the basis of a new social hierarchy. Since very few studies of this emergent panchayat social order are available, the following description should be interpreted as a preliminary evaluation based on trends in some selected areas—primarily in the eastern and central Tarai and Kathmandu valley—where rapid economic development has accelerated social changes.

Local panchayat institutions created a new, well-defined geographic basis for the interaction of village elites. Due to the changes introduced since 1975, the nine wards, each approximately equivalent to a small village, now send five elected representatives each to the panchayat assembly, which in turn elects the panchayat council and mayor (pradhan panch). Because the mayor can influence the implementation of several important government programs and development projects in the panchayat, local alliances seek control of the village panchayat elections and influence over the district-level branch of the Back-to-the-Village National Campaign Committee, which must endorse all candidates.

The elected panchayat officials do not, however, monopolize the intermediary position between village and state. Other political factions, including vestiges of the illegal political party movements, interact frequently with district-level political leaders and government officials despite their lack of official status. Previous patrons still look after the affairs of some loyal village clients. In the most sophisticated areas, villagers go directly to the relevant district administrative offices for such personal needs as citizenship papers, land-transfer registration, special loan programs, or the hundreds of other new services and obligations processed by the bureaucracy. But more frequently, specialized administrative go-betweens represent villagers in particular district offices: the village schoolteachers, local panchayat clerical staff members, elites oriented toward social work, or the professional petitioners (lekhandas) and real-estate operators. In addition, villagers may now deal with a number of merchants: a local storekeeper for short-term credit and everyday needs; a grain merchant to sell surplus food grain (which 50 percent of Tarai but only 13 percent of hill families sell); and cloth, jewelry, and other specialized itinerant merchants for particular needs. In other words, villagers tend to establish multiple special-purpose relationships beyond the village boundaries, which give them greater independence from any individual intermediary and less status inferiority in these relationships.

Changes were even more noticeable at the next higher

social level of the panchayat order, in the administrative centers of the seventy-five development districts formed in 1962. Each district, with an average population of 160,000 organized into about forty local panchayat areas, became an important social arena with a relatively stable and easily identified district elite. Particularly in the thriving, dusty, Tarai centers, the local notables met and intermingled uneasily with the central bureaucratic officers and the town's commercial and new "intellectual" elites. None of these groups had clear status superiority over the others. But since the panchayat system gave each rural panchayat one vote and only a few additional votes to the more populous towns (thereby favoring rural areas over the politically more demanding towns), the rural notables generally dominated the district panchayat. Most notables wishing to retain their status established residences in the towns despite the problems this posed in relations with other town elites and with notables from other ethnic groups. The young, educated, cosmopolitan administrative officers from Kathmandu, who have replaced the older, more conservative Rana bureaucrats, are seldom posted in one place long enough to establish close friendships with any groups in the district society. Thus the district's political and administrative elites, coming as they do from very different social milieus, maintain at best an uneasy truce. Each group perceives its own status to be relatively higher than that of other groups. Yet each group also requires cooperation from other groups, thereby increasing the importance of the locally recruited bureaucratic staff. By accepting lower status in relationships with both groups, young staff members can act as intermediaries in direct negotiations between politicians and administrators, thus avoiding the status conflicts that would hamper such negotiations.

A multitude of relationships too numerous to list here connects district-level society with important power centers in Kathmandu. Indeed, even some local panchayat elites with little influence on the district level developed direct contacts with central political and administrative elites. The improved road and air transportation system encouraged such contacts, as has the propensity of central administrators to make even the most detailed decisions about the location and execution of important local development projects. But the most fundamental reason for the greater volume and complexity of relationships between center and village has been the expanded involvement of rural groups in the panchayat system's complex set of central institutions.

The king stands at the apex of the political system, and the royal family clearly outranks all other social contenders. But below the royal family there is little agreement on the social ranking of other groups. The Ranas have lost their hegemony over official social and political rank, but the "two-hundred families," as they are sometimes called, retain considerable prestige and influence because of their wealth and education; their numerous positions in bureaucratic, political, and military institutions; and their network of client families among other political and bureaucratic elites.

Bureaucratic elites have become more powerful under the new regime because the new political leaders possess neither the administrative experience nor the established authority and social status of the former Rana leaders. On the other hand, the secretary in each ministry is formally subordinate to the cabinet minister drawn from the central political elites and ranks below him in official protocol. Status distinctions have continued within the bureaucracy between the gazetted (higher) ranks, still dominated by well-educated sons of established Brahman, Chetri, and Newar bureaucratic families in Kathmandu, and the nongazetted ranks, in which local notable families have made considerable inroads. Seldom is a nongazetted officer promoted into the gazetted ranks. Both groups are subdivided into four hierarchical rankings, and status differences between ranks are jealously guarded. As a result of the fierce competition for promotions, the need for several patrons among both bureaucratic and political elites is perhaps stronger under the present diffuse decision process than it was under the centrally controlled promotional process in the smaller Rana bureaucracy. Consequently, bureaucratic elite families have expanded their contacts to new central political leaders and even to local notables. The latter not only own land that bureaucratic families would like to share (through marriage, for example) but also can provide the intervention needed to implement local development projects and to generate support at the center for administrative promotions. Indeed, sons of some traditional bureaucratic families have entered the political arena, further blurring the distinction between bureaucratic and political elites.

Central political elites in the panchayat system fill positions in several overlapping, interconnected institutions—some very powerful, others primarily honorary—which developed, in part, to provide places for the broad spectrum of new elites recruited into the system. The National Panchayat, for example, has provided a forum in which local notables could participate regularly as members of an established central institution. The more successful members of the National Panchayat have become an established part of Kathmandu society, interacting more frequently with other central elites than with their former district clients and associates. They must, however, use their contacts with top bureaucrats and ministers on behalf of their district clients and supporters, since their clients could readily shift loyalty to other candidates in the next election.

The prime minister and his fellow cabinet ministers fill the upper echelons of the panchayat system, outranking the top bureaucrats while in office. After their generally short tenure in the cabinet, they continue to retain a VIP status and are frequently appointed to various committees and commissions. Ministers are frequently selected from important ethnic and regional groups, thus involving notables as well as more urban-oriented groups directly in cabinet-level discussions. The status of the new ministerial and panchayat elites, however, remains unsettled within the sophisticated Kathmandu society because, by necessity, these elites reflect the diverse rural cultures being integrated into the national society. Thus, by increasing participation in central institutions and reducing the monopoly of authority possessed by state agents, the emergent panchayat social order has introduced considerable status ambiguity and more diverse linkages both between different status levels and among individuals on the same level.

The incremental approach to social change evidenced in central policies since unification has laid a firm foundation for integrating Nepal's diverse population. But the ideals of egalitarian social justice and accelerated economic development, which challenged the principles of the Rana social order, have also discredited gradualist approaches to social change. Frustrated with the delays and conflicting purposes pursued by different groups and status levels even within the centrally controlled panchayat system, reformers in the central institutions have sought to circumvent the notables and village elites and to intervene directly in village affairs. But direct central intervention, which may become possible in Nepal if bureaucratic capabilities continue to improve, poses two potential threats to the emergent national society. First, the bureaucratic imperative to eliminate local variations and impose uniform norms throughout the nation threatens to destroy, in the name of social justice, the familiar customs that give life meaning for those sharing different ethnic identities. Thus, the often insensitive bureaucracy inadvertently exploits local society in pursuit of its reforms. And second, if the existing social hierarchy is successfully excluded from controls over central intervention and is allowed to atrophy, central institutions will have no intermediate institutions to fall back on when unforeseeable changes pose problems for government programs. Reform of the present hierarchy, slow and unrewarding as such a gradual undertaking is, may provide a more certain transition to the society envisioned by central reformers than wholesale attempts to destroy it and replace the present elites with new ones.

Notes

1. See Mahesh C. Regmi, *Landownership in Nepal* (Berkeley: University of California Press, 1976), for a detailed description of the tenure systems in Nepal and the role of the state agent in each system.

4

The Quest for Economic Growth

The fall of the Rana regime in 1951 stimulated a reassessment of Nepal's economic institutions. Concern with economic development took its place beside political legitimacy and social justice in the intellectual debates that flourished during the 1950s and led to a dramatic increase in the economic activities of the central government in the 1960s and 1970s.

By the beginning of the twentieth century, entrepôt trade between Tibet and British India had developed through the Chumbi valley route to the east of Nepal, leaving Nepal's economy isolated except for a small trade with India. But prospering urban markets in India and the extension of the Indian railway system to Nepal's borders created a growing demand for Nepal's rice and timber. The Rana government encouraged private investment in new Tarai settlements to develop agricultural exports, but was reluctant to open Nepal to Indian merchants and industrialists who might dominate the Nepali economy and disrupt the social order. By 1923, however, the Ranas acceded to British demands that British and Indian commodities—particularly textiles—be given access to Nepal's fledgling markets.

Cheap imports had the same disastrous effects on Nepal's thriving cottage industry that they had on home crafts everywhere in Asia. Yet the Rana government failed to provide encouragement or capital to stimulate the development of similar industries within Nepal. Only in 1936, after the first Nepal Company Act was promulgated, did the government become interested in industrial development. A few jute, cotton, textile, oil, and rice industries, established in the Tarai with the aid of

Indian businessmen, prospered because of world scarcities and high prices during World War II, but most went bankrupt with the return of normal economic conditions after the war—an ominous precedent for Nepal's potential entrepreneurs.

The quest for economic growth began in earnest after 1951, but even a brief review of the results after three decades of development effort is enough to discourage fainthearted planners. In 1978, per capita income was below $100, ranking Nepal among the poorest countries in the world.[1] Most Nepalis earn considerably less than this, since half of the national income is earned by an estimated 13 percent of the population—the wealthiest 3 percent earn more than one-fourth of the total. Of course, low per capita income in a subsistence economy may not signify an impoverished living standard if every family owns sufficient land, but the average hill family in Nepal must survive on only one acre of land—even less than in Bangladesh. Real economic growth during the past two decades averaged just slightly over 2 percent per year despite $450 million in foreign aid, as well as considerable internal investment in development programs. Since population has grown at about the same rate, per capita income has not grown at all. The modern industrial sector—the focus of most development strategies—accounts for less than 4 percent of the gross domestic product (GDP) and offers little hope for expanding employment rapidly enough to absorb the expanding labor force.

Contrary to earlier expectations, Nepal's mineral resources—primarily talc, ocher, slate, limestone (for cement), and copper—appear to be very limited and of marginal value. The mountain rivers offer tremendous hydroelectric potential, but large capital investments will be necessary before hydroelectric power can play a significant role in the economy. Tourism offers some potential of increasing foreign-exchange earnings, for tourists traveling to India have also been attracted to Nepal in increasing numbers. Tourist expenditures have risen steadily from less than $60,000 in 1960 to more than $30 million annually by 1979 (or almost 25 percent of foreign-exchange receipts), most of which remain in the Kathmandu valley.

Agriculture dominates the Nepali economy, accounting for about 65 percent of the GDP, 80 percent of total export earnings, and more than 94 percent of the labor force. Rice is planted on more than half of the 5 million acres on which food grains are grown, with lesser amounts of corn, wheat, millet, and barley sown on the rest. Another 0.5 million acres are used each year to raise cash crops, the most important of which are oilseeds, potatoes, jute, sugarcane, and tobacco.

The basic problem in agriculture is low productivity, which is caused by problems typical of subsistent peasant economies in Asia: acute population pressure on limited cultivated land, primitive production technology, lack of supply and marketing infrastructure, reliance on uncertain rainfall, and limited credit facilities to finance capital improvements and the adaptation of new technologies. Nepal does have a reserve of cultivable jungle lands to absorb some of its expanding population, but even this safety valve will likely be exhausted in another decade. One study found that annual agricultural production between 1966 and 1973 rose at only 1.2 percent despite the annual increase in cultivated area of 1.8 percent. Thus, yields actually decreased 0.2 percent annually because of initial low productivity on new lands. With production lagging behind population growth, surplus rice production for export fell from half a million metric tons in the early 1960s to less than 200,000 tons in the late 1970s.

While agricultural exports have decreased, the demand for manufactured goods, machinery, transportation equipment, and fuel for development efforts has constantly increased, and with it, the amount of imports. Thus, Nepal suffers the classical problem of developing countries; export earnings from a stagnant agricultural sector provide an insufficient base to finance the growing consumer and industrial demands for imported food and manufactured products. Nepal's landlocked geographic location magnifies this problem—first because the lack of an ocean port increases the costs and difficulties of foreign trade and second because the long open border with India, combined with considerable dependence on India for both trade and transit of overseas trade, limits the possible economic-growth strategies Nepal could pursue.

The worst economic problems are concentrated in the hill and high mountain regions, where two-thirds of Nepal's popu-

lation ekes out a living on only one-third of the nation's cultivated land. Food-grain deficits have developed in many areas,
varying between 150,000 to 200,000 metric tons annually for
the hill areas as a whole. Forest resources for fuel and cattle
forage near settlements have been depleted, pastures overgrazed,
and cultivation attempted on increasingly marginal land; resultant environmental degradation has increased the frequency of
landslides, which, in turn, have reduced available croplands.
Porters must carry supplies to most hill towns, and in some
areas even this primitive mode of transport is unavailable.
Thus, an unreliable transportation system, combined with the
subsistence-level economy, has discouraged industrial and commercial development. With no alternative source of employment
and no developed export potential, only government subsidies
and repatriated earnings from migrant labor in India or the
Tarai have enabled hill residents to buy the food grain they
need from other areas.

This bleak statistical outlook, however, does little justice
to dynamic forces evident in the economy and to the considerable progress made during the last two decades. As foreign-aid
and government development officers point out in response to
criticism, investment in needed economic infrastructure necessarily reduced public investment in more productive activities.
Nepal has expanded communication and transportation facilities linking major population centers throughout the country:
by 1970 the primitive systems relied on by the Ranas were
expanded, primarily through foreign-aid projects, to include
twenty airports, 1,384 miles of paved highway, and 2,347 miles
of unpaved roads. Commercial banks expanded from 6 branches
in 1950 to 220 in 1978. Each of the seventy-five towns designated as district administrative headquarters now has a bank as
well as numerous government offices that did not exist in 1950.

New construction has changed the face of Kathmandu,
Pokhara, and the prosperous commercial centers in the Tarai.
Boom towns filled with merchants and small service shops have
sprung up along the expanding network of roads, and rural
bazaars have expanded throughout the Tarai and in some hill
areas. Even remote hill areas interact with geographically broader
market systems, as is evident from the invasion of the ubiqui-

tous radio, wristwatch, and other symbols of modern consumer preferences. Despite gloomy statistics, Nepal has so far avoided the problems of starvation and chronic malnutrition, of disruptive urban migration and slums, and of burdensome foreign indebtedness and lack of convertible currency reserves (except for the troublesome Indian rupee) that plague other developing economies. A closer look at past developments in each sector will help clarify present problems and the policy choices made to solve them.

Agricultural-Development Strategies

The agricultural sector so dominates Nepal's economy that any major development effort must include a strategy to increase agricultural productivity. But government programs in this sector are faced with a complex mosaic of production patterns and land-tenure systems, which have evolved from historical migrations, local variations in land grants and administrative authority, and numerous climate and soil variations typical of mountainous terrain. Furthermore, by the 1950s farmers in the areas with greatest population pressure on limited cultivated land were already using available resources efficiently, given the constraints on available technology and the existing agrarian institutions. Thus the primary strategies to increase agricultural production were to expand the cultivated areas in sparsely settled areas of the Tarai, to restructure Nepal's agrarian institutions, and to introduce new technologies and new crops in appropriate areas.

The main preoccupation of the Rana government had been to convert rich forested areas of the Tarai into cropland by offering tax concessions and advantageous tenure systems to contracting agrarian entrepreneurs. Recruitment of cultivators, forest clearing, irrigation systems, roads, and export marketing arrangements were the responsibility of these private contractors, who might lose claim to the land if they failed to clear the assigned area and establish viable settlements. Stimulated by urban India's growing demand for rice, a dynamic private sector developed in which subcontractors vied for controls over land and for the most profitable tenure arrangements.

After the Rana government fell in 1950, public debate concentrated on proposed agrarian reforms to reduce the inequities and exploitation resulting from the Rana system of tax collection and contract settlements. Political instability and a weak central government, however, delayed reforms until the early 1960s. When finally implemented, these previously uncoordinated reform proposals had been integrated into a sophisticated land-reform program designed to fundamentally alter Nepal's agrarian society in order to increase both industrial and agricultural productivity.

Industrial growth was to be stimulated by transfers of resources from agriculture. Maximum land-ownership ceilings would reorient agrarian entrepreneurs toward industrial development rather than land accumulation. Above-ceiling land would be confiscated and sold by the state, the money invested in industry, and industrial shares issued as compensation for the land. Interest ceilings on agricultural loans would similarly induce rural moneylenders to invest in industry, and "compulsory savings" levied on land would generate institutional credit for both agriculture and industry. At the same time, agricultural productivity would be enhanced: cadastral surveys and land titles, by securing the rights of owners, would encourage them to improve their lands; rent limitation, allowing tenants to keep increased yields, would stimulate them to intensify cultivation practices; low rents would also encourage owners to cultivate their own land and therefore take more interest in agriculture; compulsory savings institutions would finance the use of modern inputs and capital improvements in land; and land and interest ceilings would weaken rich conservative landlords and limit their ability to oppose village development programs seeking to aid tenants and cultivators.

Despite government efforts to implement land reform, political realities, conflicting political goals, and administrative weaknesses limited the program's effectiveness. Land ceilings were set high enough not to affect many landlords, and enforcement problems limited land redistribution to token amounts in all but a few Tarai districts. Most large landowners, sufficiently uncertain about future enforcement to stop further investment in land committed their money to commerce—

particularly to high-profit smuggling—and to safer investments in India rather than to Nepal's industrial development.

Many tenants were evicted and landowners reduced in status to tenants before government surveyors arrived. Although tenants on the better Tarai- and Kathmandu-valley lands did increase yields in response to rent reduction, the increased production did not compensate for losses on the greater amount of previously tenanted land now cultivated suboptimally by landlords unwilling to accept new tenants and unable to farm efficiently. More than $10 million in compulsory savings—equivalent in the mid-1960s to three years of land revenue—were collected in cash and grain, but funds were poorly used. Less than half was employed to provide credit for farmers purchasing modern agricultural inputs; most of the rest was committed to village-level loans that have defied collection. Since the compulsory-savings village committee and the government-organized village cooperatives failed, both of which were to provide institutional loans to villagers, interest restrictions on agricultural loans, by decreasing profitability and increasing the risks in moneylending, have made it more difficult for farmers to get loans. Land reform succeeded in weakening institutions through which dominant landlords controlled the production of entire villages, but it failed to establish new institutions that would provide credit, marketing, and irrigation facilities for the new "middle-class" owner-cultivators and registered tenants.

The land-reform program did, however, create a relatively uniform modern system of landownership and tax administration to replace the previous patchwork of tenure systems. Better records improved the security of registered tenants and owners and provided the basis for mortgage-oriented institutional credit necessary for specialized agricultural projects. Government registration of land sales stimulated the commercialization of land, particularly in the Tarai, and accelerated the replacement of resource-poor, isolated tribal cultivators by richer, aggressive cultivators more closely attuned to national policies. Distributive questions aside, the program created more economic dislocation and greater agrarian unrest than was justified by these minimal achievements. (Some landlords were hurt and some tenants helped, but most gains and losses affected the distribution of income among ethnic groups as much as among different levels of the social hierarchy.)

After a few turbulent years of land reform in the mid-1960s, government programs shifted emphasis to less disruptive agricultural extension efforts to introduce new "green revolution" technology. Nepal had begun a small community-development program in the late 1950s modeled after a similar program in India. When Nepal adopted a foreign aid–financed program based on improved grain varieties, chemical fertilizer, and controlled cultivation techniques, the community-development orientation changed to a narrower focus on agricultural extension. By 1970, more than 1,200 trained village agents had been posted throughout the country; the Agricultural Supply Corporation had distributed seeds of improved varieties, fertilizer, and pesticides at subsidized prices; and various schemes had been introduced to help farmers finance expensive modern cultivation practices.

The green revolution achieved notable success in the Kathmandu valley and some areas in the east Tarai. But imported varieties did well only under certain conditions and required large quantities of fertilizer, irrigation water, and pesticides at the proper time. Unreliable supplies and uncontrolled conditions made the new varieties too risky for most Nepali farmers, who lacked food reserves to support themselves in case of crop failure. In addition, green revolution technologies channeled government resources away from the acute agricultural problems in the hills, since the rich Tarai area was best suited for the new programs. Finally, these programs emphasized basic food grains and ignored the development of a more diversified, export-oriented cash-crop sector, thereby continuing Nepal's dependence on rice and jute exports.

In the early 1970s, government efforts shifted to an emphasis on horticultural and animal-husbandry projects designed to benefit the hill areas. Agricultural commodities appropriate for export to the Tarai and India, such as fruits, spices, and medicinal herbs, could help hill areas pay for the growing food-grain imports. But the hills have special problems. Intensive cultivation techniques already use available resources as efficiently as is practicable. Modern agriculture aids would be costly to transport to hill farms, and land for new crops would leave less land for food grains. International research has not focused on hill agriculture, and Nepali research efforts have to contend with a wide range of microclimates, which limits the applicability of new discoveries. Thus, progress in hill areas will not be spectacular, although it may eventually expand existing production of goods for the export market.

Agricultural policies have also encouraged a shift in the Tarai to cash crops and to export production. Foreign-aid programs have provided technical expertise, credit, and marketing facilities to increase the quality and quantity of sugarcane, cotton, jute, and tobacco production and to establish processing plants. Government-controlled companies have also been established to export rice and jute, although they initially functioned primarily to control smuggling and probably reduced exports. Government agencies have attempted to set grading standards for rice and other products to assure the quality necessary to compete in overseas markets.

Finally, a higher priority has been given to irrigation. Several major river projects have been planned, which, when completed, will fully irrigate almost 10 percent of Nepal's cultivated land, doubling the area presently supplied by minor irrigation systems dependent on rain and underground water. Preliminary discussions of the sixth plan have proposed that irrigation facilities be constructed by 1985 to service 40 percent of the Tarai and 25 percent of the hill-area fields—overly optimistic, perhaps, but indicative of the high priority given to irrigation.

The most impressive agricultural achievement in the past few decades, however, took place with almost no direct government involvement. Since 1960, a massive exodus of more than 500,000 hill farmers and dependents cleared and illegally settled more than 450,000 acres of Tarai jungle. During the same period, government resettlement projects, bogged down by funding problems, bureaucratic infighting, and conflicting political demands, cleared and settled less than one-twentieth that amount in the same general area. Privately organized groups receiving no government subsidies thus expanded Nepal's cultivated area by more than 10 percent, relieving in the process some of the population pressure in the hills.

This migration was encouraged indirectly by two government programs: the successful malaria-eradication program, which removed the major impediment to all previous attempts to coax hill settlers into the Tarai, and the construction of the Mahendra (east-west) Highway at the foot of the hills, which encouraged hill residents to develop new villages in jungle areas near the road despite the loosely enforced government ban on unauthorized settlements. Unlike earlier contract-settlement efforts, the cultivators themselves organized and financed many of these settlements, although moneylending practices and land swindles have caused serious ownership disputes between cultivators and other claimants. Perhaps twice the already resettled area remains for future settlements, but the government has established stricter controls since the early 1970s to preserve valuable jungle resources as well as to reduce conflicts over ownership. Although these controls may be necessary, the migration stands as a tribute to the continuing dynamism in Nepal's private agricultural sector and as a challenge to arguments favoring more centralized bureaucratic controls over the economy.

Foreign-Trade and Industrial-Growth Strategies

Nepal's industrial growth is inextricably linked to its foreign-trade policies not only because larger markets are needed to stimulate industrialization, but also because Nepal must import even basic industrial inputs such as steel, cement, petroleum, and machinery. Furthermore, the dominant influence of the Indian economy on Nepal has restricted the choices open to Nepali economic leaders and has caused rapid changes in policies at times so as to adjust to or counteract political and economic trends in India. Over 90 percent of Nepal's trade is with India, compared to less than 1 percent with China, Nepal's neighbor to the north. Thus trade and industrial-growth strategies have continued to be conditioned by Nepali fears of domination by the political and economic elites of its neighbor to the south.

Nepal's current trade and industrial-development problems trace their origins to the period following Indian independence, when Prime Minister Nehru's government adopted an import-substitution development policy that placed high tariffs on imports from industrialized countries in order to promote domestic industrialization. The 1950 Nepal-India treaty, signed during the last days of the Rana regime, essentially made Nepal an extension of the protected Indian market. Trade between the two countries was unrestricted, but Nepal's import and export tariffs on overseas trade had to equal the Indian tariffs in order for Nepal to enjoy unrestricted transit rights through India. India insisted on equal tariffs to prevent Nepal from importing goods at low world-market prices and selling them in India's protected market.

Unfortunately, this strategy did not spur industrial development in Nepal. Poor transportation facilities, the lack of prosperous urban markets, and the segmented, largely nonmonetized rural markets discouraged industrialists wishing to cater exclusively to the Nepali market. In addition, the more established input markets, financial institutions, trained labor force, and channels of distribution in India put potential Nepali manufacturers at a distinct disadvantage in their competition with goods produced in India, whether sold in India or Nepal. And since the commercial linkages between hill areas and the railheads built by Indian railroads at regular intervals along the border had rendered other trade routes within Nepal obsolete, a Nepali manufacturer faced a disadvantage in competing with Indian goods even in adjoining districts within Nepal. Furthermore, political agitation against the Ranas and their allies, the wealthiest group of potential entrepreneurs in Nepal, encouraged them to invest in India, not Nepal. Indian industrialists, similarly, were discouraged from making long-term investments in Nepal by political instability, administrative incompetence, and uncertainty over economic policies. As a consequence, Nepali consumers were indirectly subsidizing industrial growth in India by paying the import-substitution prices for Indian goods.

The Trade and Transit Treaty of 1960, recognizing some of the injustices in the earlier treaty, allowed Nepal to pursue an independent economic policy geared to the specific needs of its economy. Signed during a period of relative trust between India and the elected Nepali Congress government, the treaty permitted Nepal to establish protective tariffs on selected Indian imports. Imports required for Nepal's development program could be procured overseas at world-market prices and transported duty free through India. Nepal was also permitted to establish its own foreign-currency reserve, thereby ending the Indian government's direct control over its foreign-trade accounts.

Unfortunately, relations between Nepal and India deteriorated shortly after the treaty was signed when the king arrested members of the Nepali Congress regime and resumed direct rule. India not only permitted the Congress party to organize opposition to the royal regime from Indian territory, but also temporarily restricted trade with Nepal to bring economic pressure on the king to accept a compromise settlement with the opposition. As a consequence, the fears of domination by merchants and industrialists from the south, which had previously prompted Rana isolationism, returned in full force. The economic strategy that evolved under the royal regime gave high priority to increasing the independence of Nepal's economy from Indian influence through policies of import substitution, trade diversification, and investment restrictions.

In Nepal's import-substitution policies during the early 1960s, foreign aid was used to develop public-sector industries to reduce imports of Indian sugar, cigarettes, shoes, and agricultural tools. The government established industrial parks and provided loans and consultants through the Nepal Industrial Development Corporation in order to encourage Nepali entrepreneurs to produce needed consumer goods for Nepal's small but expanding population centers. The 1975–1980 five-year plan continued to emphasize the need for complementary economies and increased trade between hill and Tarai areas within Nepal in order to reduce the need for Indian imports in both regions.

Trade-diversification policies were designed to alter Nepal's almost exclusive trade with India by encouraging trade with other nations as well. But these policies faced two serious problems. First, since all but the most valuable commodities that could be airfreighted had to be shipped overland to and from Indian ports, overseas trade from Nepal faced relatively high transportation costs. These added costs reduced the potential advantage Nepal's export sector may have had in overseas markets and made Indian markets the most logical target for most programs to expand exports. Second, since India could still disrupt overseas trade by restricting the transit of goods through India, the Nepali economy remained vulnerable to Indian pressures.

The royal regime partially overcame these problems by exploiting the 1960 treaty's guaranteed right of unrestricted transit in order to subsidize overseas exports. Nepal allowed Indian firms to build several final-processing plants just inside the border, which used low-duty imported stainless steel and synthetic fabrics and exported the products duty free into the protected Indian markets, thereby earning immense profits (and undermining India's import-substitution policy). Traders were also allowed to import luxury consumer items from overseas, which were illegally distributed in Indian black markets by well-organized smuggling operations. In order to import the stainless steel, synthetic fabrics, and luxury goods from overseas, however, traders had to export Nepali products to earn import entitlements—at times jute, the major hard-currency earner, was even smuggled into Nepal from India and sold on the world market at only 50 percent of its procurement price, an indication of the profitability of the imports. By giving a higher percentage of import entitlements for designated categories of exports, the government directed these unofficial export subsidies toward handicrafts and processed goods and away from unprocessed agricultural products. Later, partly in response to Indian pressure, Nepal limited luxury imports to a small fraction of the value of the import entitlement and required the rest to be used to import development materials.

Unfortunately, the open border that encouraged smuggling to support Nepal's trade-diversification policy worked against other economic policies. Smugglers also shipped Nepal's subsidized fertilizer, sugar, and foodstuffs into higher-priced Indian markets, rendering Nepali price stabilization and use-incentive programs ineffective. Similarly, Nepal canceled high protective tariffs several times because the consequent smuggling decreased customs revenue without significantly reducing Indian imports. Although the profit from such minor smuggling was insignificant compared to the unofficially estimated $50 million in luxury goods annually smuggled into India, the volume at times was more impressive—e.g., high Indian prices in 1973 attracted an estimated 120,000 tons of illegally exported rice from Nepal. But the difficulty of policing the long border and the greater problem of controlling corruption has discouraged both India and Nepal from imposing more restrictive border controls to prevent smuggling.

Finally, Nepal used investment restrictions to prevent Indian industrialists from dominating Nepal's growing industrial sector. The 1974 Industrial Enterprises Act extended previous limitations by reserving for the government controlling shares in large power, metals, chemicals, and basic consumer industries. All foreign (that is, Indian) ownership of small industry was forbidden, and Nepali applicants for licenses to open medium-sized industries (1 to 5 million rupees) were given preference over foreigners. Foreign applicants were at least formally given equal opportunity on large investments, perhaps because Nepali investments of that magnitude were unlikely. Restrictions prevented most industrial development within five miles of the border, where Indians might gain most controls and benefits. Despite these and earlier restrictions, at least 75 percent of Nepal's industrial investment and most industrial employment have been located in the Tarai. Plants are generally managed and even owned by Indians through Nepali intermediaries and employ skilled Indian workers. Despite the economic utility of these immigrants—especially given the shortage of skilled Nepali workers, managers, and entrepreneurs—the government has imposed restrictive policies on immigration in an attempt to increase the demand for industrial skills and employment among its own citizens. The legal difficulty in distinguishing between Nepali citizens in the Tarai and their noncitizen brethren across the border, however, has made enforcement of discriminatory measures less effective. And bureaucratic controls that harass noncitizens have a way of discouraging Nepali entrepreneurs as well.

India accepted Nepal's independent economic policies with restraint in the 1960s but reacted more negatively during the 1970s. The Trade and Transit Treaty of 1971, signed only after long, tedious negotiations, reaffirmed in principle Nepal's right to set independent tariff schedules and to transport overseas trade through India, but in effect made transit rights dependent on Nepal's efforts to restrict smuggling operations based in Nepal. India imposed export quotas on certain development materials in short supply, partly out of concern that Nepal's purchases would end up in the Indian black markets. Later, when Nepal sought overseas contracts to replace higher-priced Indian imports, India began charging international prices for other goods previously supplied at subsidized domestic prices. In the period following the 1973 Arab oil boycott, for example, India supplied oil products to Nepal at domestic prices well below what India had paid to import the oil. India later demanded, however, that Nepal pay the international price in foreign exchange rather than, as previously, in Indian rupees.

Overall, Nepal's efforts to stimulate industrial growth while developing an independent economy have been partially rewarded. The industrial sector's contribution to the GNP increased from 1.4 percent in 1965 to 3 percent a decade later. Production capacity increased even more, but underutilization of capacity in most large plants, particularly in the stainless-steel and now defunct synthetic-textile plants, led to sluggish growth in production. Most public corporations were also producing very low returns on government investments. Trade-diversification policies succeeded in expanding officially recorded non-Indian trade from 3 percent in 1960 to more than 25 percent in recent years, but overseas trade probably constitutes no more than 10 percent of Nepal's total trade when illegal trade figures are added in. Moreover, much of the trade with third countries is still dependent on profits earned from smuggling operations into India. Total trade has more than quadrupled during this time, but exports have consistently earned less than two-thirds of Nepal's import bill, leaving a trade deficit in fiscal 1976 of $67 million. Although foreign aid, Indian excise-tax refunds, earnings from tourism, and repatriated earnings from smuggling and employment in India have enabled Nepal to balance its payments and maintain a foreign-currency reserve equal in 1978 to about nine months of imports, the balance has become more precarious in recent years. Since critical construction and development goods must be imported, and since Nepali consumers spend an estimated 40 percent of any increase in income on imported goods, the lagging export sector has become a major obstacle to economic growth.

In 1978, continuing concern over trade deficits and improvements in overall relations with India brought a reevaluation of Nepal's independent economic policies and a dramatic shift toward economic cooperation with India. After long negotiations, separate trade and transit treaties and a Memorandum of Understanding on Industrial and Economic Cooperation were signed with India, which satisfied Nepal's demands for symbols of independence as well as India's demands for effective smuggling controls, setting the stage for further cooperation. Since then, both sides have shown signs of greater willingness to cooperate. Talks have resumed on several joint hydroelectric projects (Nepal's potential is estimated to be greater than the installed capacity of Mexico, Canada, and the United States combined). These projects could help control flooding and supply irrigation and much of the power needs for northern India, while providing cheap electricity, irrigation, and foreign exchange for Nepal. Furthermore, India published a long list of Nepali goods that could enter Indian markets with no restrictions and discussed possible railroad linkages with industrial locations within Nepal. Nepal has actively courted public and private Indian involvement in comprehensive plans to establish industries in Nepal capable of penetrating established Indian markets. And finally, Nepal has altered its policies and, more importantly, its enforcement of antismuggling laws. In the last weeks of 1978, several ministers and more than twenty top administrative officials were suddenly removed from office because of their role in smuggling-related activities such as the overinvoicing of exports and underinvoicing of imports.[2] Since these activities were commonplace even before the present officials had assumed their positions and had been known to the palace for more than a decade, the sudden crackdown represented a dramatic shift in Nepal's trade policies, not simply the aftermath of an isolated scandal.

Despite the problems of insuring that industries established under the new policy are integrated into the economy and not just isolated Indian enclaves in Nepal, the present leaders in Kathmandu have apparently resigned themselves to the need for Indian industrialists' greater participation in Nepal's economic development. If this mood continues, Nepal's increasingly sophisticated bureaucracy may be able to bargain for specific benefits (i.e., job-training programs for Nepali workers) without completely discouraging Indian investments as it has in the past. The new policies may also attract a new kind of Indian investor interested in projects with long-term viability rather than in short-term profits based on smuggling. Critical negotiations lie ahead, but if economic growth rather than economic independence remains the major concern in future discussions, the controlled influx of Indian investments, entrepreneurship, and organizations may stimulate Nepal's sluggish industrial growth.

Government Economic Activities

Since Nepal, like most developing countries, has relied on centrally directed, bureaucratically controlled development strategies, the government itself has been the most rapidly expanding sector in the economy. Total government expenditures increased from $21 million in fiscal 1963 (1963–1964) to an estimated $300 million in fiscal 1978 (1978–1979); even discounting for inflation (consumer prices have almost doubled during the last decade), real expenditures have grown steadily at almost 20 percent annually. During the decade following 1963, government expenditures rose from less than 5 percent to more than 9 percent of the GDP and have continued to climb since then. The government employs more of the labor force than the entire modern industrial sector and accounts for almost all white-collar jobs. In addition, the demand for government employee housing and office space has created a construction boom in administrative centers throughout the country, stimulating considerable private investment in urban properties.

Even before 1950, the government had experimented with more direct involvement in the economy and even considered formulating a national economic plan. But Nepal's major expansion of public-sector activities began with the first five-year plan covering the period from 1956 to 1960. Rudimentary economic statistics were gathered for the first time to assess economic bottlenecks and to target government expenditures. Although the plans seldom were consulted when project expenditures were approved, the planning mechanism created a new "development" budget that roughly monitored the growing economic (as opposed to defense, law-and-order, and general administration) functions of the government. The development budget grew even more rapidly than general expenditures, from an annual average budget of $3.4 million during the first plan to $220 million in fiscal 1978, constituting 70 percent of that year's total expenditure. Expenditures averaging $320 million annually at present price levels are being projected for the sixth five-year plan (1980–1985), indicating that government economic programs will continue their rapid expansion.

Fully 80 percent of development expenditures since 1955 was spent to improve Nepal's basic economic infrastructure (roads, airports, financial institutions, and so on), which had been ignored by the Rana regime, while less than 20 percent was spent on programs directly related to increasing production. Almost half the total expenditure went to the transportation and communication sector, primarily to the major foreign-aid road-construction projects. Although only 28 percent of the current plan expenditures is allotted to this sector, several major road projects under discussion in 1979 might boost actual expenditures well above the planned level. Agricultural and rural development projects steadily increased their share of expenditures from 20 percent in the first plan to 30 percent in the current plan, whereas the industrial sector has averaged only 5 percent since the beginning. Expenditures for education, health, and other social services declined from 18 percent of the first plan to 14 percent of the third, but increased steadily to a projected 22 percent for the fifth plan period (1975–1980).

The rapid expansion of development expenditures has been encouraged and supported by foreign aid, which contributed more than half the development expenditures between 1963 and 1972 and is expected to finance more than 40 percent of the sixth five-year plan. In the early 1960s, when aid contributed up to two-thirds of the annual development outlays, Nepal could not even use all available aid: the inexperienced administration could neither develop projects fast enough nor spend the approved funds on schedule. Aid donors from almost every aid-giving nation, including Nepal's "underdeveloped" neighbors, India and China, vied with each other to gain approval for their pet projects and to secure scarce Nepali administrative talent to implement them. Although this competition suited the royal regime's foreign policy and inadvertently produced an experimental approach to development more suitable for Nepal's uncharted economy than formalized national planning, the resultant confusion weakened the planners' efforts to coordinate overall growth.

There were few trained economic planners in Nepal in the 1960s, and the institutional basis for their operation, which shifted between a National Planning Commission outside the Central Secretariat and an Economic Planning Ministry within the bureaucracy, gave them little control over the government's actual expenditure. The number of trained economists and policy planners increased significantly, however, because of numerous educational exchange programs, providing enough manpower by the mid-1970s to staff separate policy planning and analysis divisions in the palace and most ministries as well as several independent policy institutions—the Centre for Economic Development and Administration, the Agricultural Projects Center, Industrial Services Center, and so on. The National Planning Commission, which since 1973 has operated ostensibly according to the directives issued by the politically oriented National Development Council, has significantly improved its analytic capabilities and coordination mechanisms to secure broader bureaucratic involvement in the preparation of five-year plans. Even more significantly, the commission has become involved in preparing annual-plan supplements based on the five-year plan and monitoring the progress of ministries in achieving these annual goals. Despite these improvements, the five-year plan remains at best a very rough estimate of available governmental resources and a catalog of policy aspirations rather than a reliable guide for the allocation of government funds.

The major spending decisions are made of necessity in the annual budgeting process or, more accurately, in the finance ministry's quarterly transfer of funds to projects on the basis of their budget allocations and previous performance. Even within these three-month time periods, uncertainties about actual revenues collected and funds already spent have posed difficult problems for the Ministry of Finance. Budgeting and accounting techniques were severely strained by the rapid expansion of field-office activities throughout the country during the 1960s. The combination of inexperienced field officers, untried programs, unsupportive central administrators, inflexible auditing practices, underdeveloped local economies, and inordinate delays in transferring approved funds to field offices enabled the average development project to spend only about two-thirds of its available funds. Gradual improvements in budgeting procedures and administrative skills have reduced some of these spending problems, but the uncertainties in estimating Nepal's volatile revenues (particularly from trade tariffs and foreign aid) and the inevitable politically expedient adjustments in the budget still limit the utility of the annual budget—let alone the five-year plan—in directing government expenditure.

By the 1970s Nepal's spending capacity was growing faster than aid contributions, particularly since the costs and salaries required to maintain aid-funded projects completed in the 1960s alone added automatic increases to the basic development budget. Furthermore, increasing reliance on multinational agencies and more stringent requirements in recent bilateral aid programs shifted the primary burden for local costs of new aid projects to Nepal. The loan component of foreign aid, negligible before 1970, increased to 55 percent of total aid financing in the 1978 budget. Since aid has become more "expensive," Nepal has become more selective about aid projects. In contrast to earlier policies, the government is now encouraging donors to coordinate their projects through an Aid Nepal Consortium, which in the late 1970s accounted for 80 percent of Nepal's aid receipts.

Although foreign aid played an indispensable role in stimulating initial development expenditures, domestic revenues have increased at a faster pace than aid grants, growing from $13 million in 1963 to a projected $166 million in fiscal 1978 (aid grants grew from $8 million to $58 million during the same period). Customs duties remain the largest component of domestic revenues, accounting for 35 to 40 percent of the total despite losses (primarily on import duty) due to smuggling and underreporting of import valuations. Revenues have increased from all tax sources, although in the mid-1960s agricultural land taxes decreased in relative importance from 26 percent of all revenues to only 6 percent in 1978. The government has improved the efficiency of its tax-collection system and has instituted several new taxes; the progressive income tax, for example, grew from under 5 percent of total revenue in 1971 to more than 12 percent in 1977.

Revenues have not, however, kept up with expenditures. Since the early 1970s, expenditures have exceeded income from revenues and aid grants by an additional $8 million each year. The estimated fiscal 1978 deficit amounted to $84 million, or about one-fourth of total expenditures. Thus Nepal has increasingly resorted to deficit financing through printing money and raising loans, particularly international loans. Since Nepal has one of the lowest international debts among developing countries—$50 million, payments on which equal only 2.4 percent of the nation's export earnings—it appears likely that it will use these loans to meet present spending demands without confronting political resistance to higher taxes. Other techniques for deficit financing have greater limits in Nepal. Printing money is not only inflationary, but also adds to consumer demand for Indian imports, thereby exacerbating the balance-of-payments problem. Domestic borrowing potential is limited, and government competition for private-sector funds would drive up interest rates and slow private investments. But international borrowing is advantageous only if government projects in fact stimulate exports and economic growth enough to cover the interest payments.

Public-sector investments to date have not been encouraging. Most projects have suffered from numerous delays and disappointing results. Nepal has approximately thirty-three public enterprises that perform economic services, but only the banks have established a reputation for profitable and efficient management. Even including the banks, the annual rate of return on assets for the twelve major enterprises that have published financial reports averaged less than 2 percent during the 1960s (when figures were available). But if the government

seriously embarks on the long-term economic-growth policies
introduced in 1978 (including a program to improve the performance of public enterprises) and carefully selects and imple-
ments public-sector projects with potentially adequate rates
of return, the low-interest rates available on international
development loans may justify the government's deficit-spending
policies.

The Political Economy of Development Strategies

Government development strategies have increased the
scope of traditional political controls over the wealth and well-
being of groups and individuals in Nepal. Elite families always
competed for government land grants, administrative positions,
and trade monopolies, which could enhance their wealth and
establish their dominance for several generations. Now industrial
licenses and loans, agricultural inputs, and the location of roads,
administrative centers, and numerous development projects
have been added to the potential rewards for political power.
Individuals and groups naturally seek development policies that
would enhance their resources: Tarai farmers seek unrestricted
trade with India while hill and urban residents seek curbs on
food exports to keep domestic prices lower; Newar merchants
who dominate hill bazaars prefer development policies aiding
hill areas, while the plains merchants who dominate Tarai
bazaars and trade with India seek infrastructural developments
in the Tarai and expanded trade with India; political and administrative groups who have shared the profits of the illicit
trade with India prefer trade-diversification policies over common tariff policies with India.

As in all countries, the distributive implications of a
proposed development policy are generally more important in
getting the policy approved and implemented than its potential
contribution to economic development. Thus it is not surprising that government investments have favored the Kathmandu
valley and the eastern Tarai, the two most sophisticated and
active political areas in Nepal. Nor is it surprising that the
government has chosen public-sector development and strict
controls over economic activities. The two rulers whose influ-

ence over policy matters since 1960 has been decisive have preferred a weak, dispersed economic elite (e.g., a public-sector
elite subject to dismissal). Foreign aid has supported and paid
for expanded bureaucratic involvement in economic activities.
In addition, the powerful bureaucratic elites in Kathmandu
have wished to gain greater control over the tremendous economic potential in the Tarai rather than let it be developed
privately by local Tarai elites. And similarly, the hill elites to
whom the monarch appealed for support after 1960 have preferred government controls that would give them an advantage
over established Tarai elites in competition for Tarai resources.
These same alliances, plus the supporters of Indian merchant
groups who profited from illicit trade, also tended to favor the
restrictive trade policies with India.

Such alignments have hampered attempts to readjust past
policies even when critical problems have emerged. King Birendra's plan since 1972 to distribute government projects on a
geographically more equitable basis has encountered considerable difficulty, both in gaining bureaucratic support to
design and implement policies in isolated areas and in controlling new demands from the well-established lobbies for existing programs in more economically advanced areas. Thus the
success of the king's hill-oriented development programs will
depend in part on his ability to strengthen political groups
(supportive of the monarchy) capable of promoting economic
activities in these areas and competing with established interest
groups for a share of government resources. Five-year plans and
even annual budgets controlled by the center, no matter how
well designed in economic terms, cannot successfully alter budget allocations without the aid of such political support.

Although not necessarily conducive to optimal choices for
economic-development strategies, the dominant role of politics
in controlling economic policy may be advantageous in a country with Nepal's poorly developed economic base and low level
of institutional development. The pursuit of economically
optimal policies that disrupt Nepal's ongoing integration processes might lead to disastrous future problems. But the importance of political factors in policy decisions poses a dilemma
for Nepal's economic policymakers: state controls are necessary
to direct entrepreneurial energy into activities with broader

long-term economic benefits for Nepal than the exploitative monopolistic practices that have predominated in the past. However, reliance on state economic controls encourages dominant groups and individuals to subvert policies through political pressure or corruption for personal gain. To escape this dilemma, at least some influential policymakers concluded by 1978 that development policies should give greater responsibility to the private sector. Where competitive market conditions control the private sector, the removal of politically exploitable state controls may result in a better allocation of resources and more dynamic management of economic enterprises. If the state continues to develop more subtle financial regulation of the economy in place of the clumsier, more restrictive direct-licensing and investment controls that have hampered development in the past, and if the goal of economic development rather than economic independence guides policy choice, the next decade may witness the substantial economic growth that has so far eluded the state-dominated economy.

Notes

1. Throughout this chapter all data originally published in Nepali rupees have been converted to U.S. dollars, using the 1978 conversion rate of 12.5 rupees per dollar. Exchange rates have varied during the period under discussion, but the use of a single conversion rate provides a more consistent basis for illustrating trends in Nepal's financial situation.

2. The extent to which overseas trade figures have been inflated by the practice of illegal overinvoicing (reporting higher values on export invoices in order to gain higher import entitlements) was reported in the *Nepal Times* on January 30, 1979—jute worth $250 to $300 per ton was invoiced at $500 to $750, tea worth $0.80 per kilogram was invoiced at $6 per kilogram, and herbs and drugs were overinvoiced by as much as 1,000 percent. Similarly, approximately $100 million worth of polyester fabric was imported between 1970 and 1976 but was generally invoiced at less than 1 percent of its actual value. By underinvoicing, importers not only could import substantially more than was justified by their import entitlements but also avoided about $100 million in import duties (*Nepal Press Digest* 23, nos. 6–7 [February 5, 12, 1979]).

5

International Relations: A Root Between Two Stones

Small countries situated in highly strategic areas between larger and more powerful neighbors must, by necessity, formulate strategies and policies that reduce their vulnerability and exploit opportunities. In crisis situations, the objective is not merely the advancement of national interests but, not infrequently, the survival of the society as an independent polity. Nepal finds itself in this unfortunate situation. On several occasions it has had to face external threats in which the absorption of the central Himalayan region by political systems to the north or south appeared to be the issue at stake. Kathmandu's responses have generally been determined by the demands of the moment as perceived by the governing elite; however, a Nepali world view, derived from decades of contentious existence in an unhealthy environment, is also evident in the definition of policies.

The strategies available to countries in Nepal's geostrategic situation are limited in number: isolation from the surrounding world to the greatest extent possible, acceptance of a subordinate position to the dominant power in the region, or a delicate exercise in the balancing off of surrounding powers in order to limit their capacity to interfere. Kathmandu has used all three strategies and, on occasion, combinations of strategies (e.g., isolation plus a subordinate status to British India), shifting back and forth as the need has arisen. The result has been a broadly based consensus within the political public in Nepal on the objectives of foreign policy, combined with vociferous debates on the proper strategy to be employed at any point in

117

time. Thus, it is necessary to understand Nepali perceptions of their historical experiences, including the more recent, to make sense out of their responses to contemporary challenges.

A central Himalayan (i.e., Nepali) world view is a relatively recent phenomenon. The Malla Kingdoms of Kathmandu had been adroit in manipulating the small but troublesome principalities that surrounded the valley and in protecting their lucrative stake in the trans-Himalayan trade system. Nothing that might be called a policy for the central Himalayas as a region, however, had ever been defined. It was only with the unification of Nepal under the Shah dynasty that regional policies and strategies were carefully devised with the interests of the central Himalayas, and not just the Kathmandu valley, in mind.

This coincided with, indeed was inspired by, significant changes in the politics of the entire Himalayan region. Prior to the late eighteenth century, there had been occasions when the Kashmir valley and western Himalayas had been arenas of contention between powerful forces in India and central Asia, but the areas of the Himalayas to the east had been relatively immune from external intervention and dominance. The central Himalayas retained their unique mixture of Hindu and Buddhist cultures intact during those difficult centuries, and the innumerable principalities in this area could carry on their internecine conflicts with little concern for the massive upheavals that periodically engulfed neighboring areas to the south. Even the powerful Moghul Empire, which brought most of the subcontinent under its control from the sixteenth to the eighteenth century and was deeply involved in Kashmir and some sections of the western Himalayas, for the most part ignored the central and eastern Himalayas, posing no problems for their security and political systems at that time.

Policies and strategies specifically directed at countering perceived threats from areas to the north and south of the central Himalayas evolved only in the latter half of the eighteenth century when the geostrategic situation in this entire region was drastically altered by several developments. The first was the emergence of a unified state, with exuberant expansionist ambitions and capabilities, under the Gorkha dynasty in Nepal. Another was the establishment of the Ch'ing dynasty as a potent factor in Tibetan politics; for the first time, China was an important ingredient in Himalayan region politics. Finally, there was the gradual extension of control by the British East India Company over the section of north India bordering on Nepal. This posed a different kind of problem for Kathmandu from that presented by the Moghuls, for the British had both economic and political interests in the trans-Himalayan region that required some form of involvement in developments in Nepal. The Chinese presence in Tibet also changed the strategic environment for the dominant power in India—at least potentially—by making the central Himalayas a primary focus of their interaction.

The Gorkha dynasty's response to this novel geostrategic development was classic for small powers in a buffer-region system. Using a metaphor of Nepal as a root between two stones, the founder of the unified Nepali state, Prithvi Narayan Shah, advised his successors to avoid entanglements with either the Chinese or the British. If this was not possible, then the two powers should be played off against each other, a strategy Nepal adopted with some success up until the mid-nineteenth century. In the 1791–1792 war with China, for instance, Kathmandu appealed to the British for military assistance; whereas in the 1814–1816 war with the British, the Nepalis sought both material and political assistance from Peking. As a corollary strategy, Nepal also adopted a strict isolationist policy directed at minimizing the capacity of and the need for either the British or the Chinese to intervene in the central Himalayas. Though this particular term was not used, Kathmandu's objective was the "neutralization" of Nepal from threatening developments in surrounding areas. Nepal also had to substitute a defensive strategy for the expansionist policies followed up to 1816, reverting to earlier form only when opportunities presented themselves.

By the mid-nineteenth century, the international situation in the Himalayan regions forced Kathmandu to revise its broader security strategy. China's virtual withdrawal as a significant factor in this region and the acceptance of the British as the paramount power by the numerous Indian princely polities made the old balancing-of-powers approach inoperative. Kathmandu

adopted the only alternative policy that made survival possible—
an accommodation with the British on the best possible terms.
This was achieved over several decades of cautious but generally
friendly interaction between the Nepalis and British, culminating eventually in a working relationship that was close, with
both sides exercising restraint while indulging in profuse expres-
sions of mutual admiration. The net effect in Nepal was to protect the Rana regime from both its internal and external enemies
without compromising the autonomy of the state on internal
matters. The British, meanwhile, obtained an invaluable support
force for their Indian empire and other colonial territories elsewhere in Asia through the recruitment of Gurkhas into the
British Indian army.

This mutually advantageous "special relationship" was
inherited by independent India after the British withdrawal
from the subcontinent in 1947, and New Delhi moved quickly
to expand and formalize the existing ties with Kathmandu.
After an initial hesitation, the Rana regime responded positively
by "lending" the Indian government several Nepali military
units during a serious crisis in 1948 and by accepting Indian
"advisers" in the formulation of a liberalized political system.
This policy of mutual accommodation was formalized on July
31, 1950, when treaties of "peace and friendship" and "trade
and commerce" were signed by the two powers. The most important feature of the first treaty was contained in a secret
letter of exchange, which stated: "Neither Government shall
tolerate any threat to the security of the other by a foreign
aggressor. To deal with any such threat the two Governments
shall consult with each other and *devise effective counter-
measures*" (emphasis added). As interpreted by both sides, this
made Nepal an integral part of the Indian security system on
the Himalayan frontier. The trade treaty included some concessions to Nepal but in fact constituted a limited common-market
agreement that exposed Nepal to various forms of Indian economic and political pressure.

The Special Relationship with India

In the fall of 1950, several events occurred in the Himalayan areas that led eventually to major political changes in Nepal. The first was the Chinese invasion of Tibet, accompanied by Chinese assertions of their intent to incorporate this "traditional Chinese territory" into their new people's empire. This forced New Delhi to abandon the strategies adopted earlier to maintain Tibet as a buffer between India and China; in the process, the Indians also had to revise their policies toward the border states to the south of the Himalayan crest. In Nepal this took the form of a decision that the Rana regime—assumed to be vulnerable to Communist subversion—had to be replaced by a more representative and modern political system. New Delhi still hoped to avoid immediate and drastic changes, but steps in the direction of a more liberal polity were considered necessary. The Indian embassy in Kathmandu arranged for the "escape" of King Tribhuvan to India in November 1950 and his establishment as an alternative to the Ranas. The various Nepali oppositionist factions that had combined into the Nepali Congress party in early 1950 were allowed to acquire arms from unofficial sources (Kashmir and Burma primarily), to set up bases in Indian territory adjacent to Nepal, and finally in November to launch a series of armed attacks against Nepal government centers in the Tarai and lower hill areas. The eventual consequence was the Delhi Compromise of February 1951 under which the Ranas, King Tribhuvan, and the Nepali Congress agreed to the formation of a coalition cabinet that would operate under the general supervision of King Tribhuvan. India, as the intermediary in these negotiations, had actually devised this formula and assumed a broad level of responsibility for its implementation. This had the effect of placing all the participants in the new government in a position of dependence upon India.

Nepal's foreign policy, as defined by India in the post-1951 period, had several basic features. The first of these was the wholesale adoption of the Indian version of nonalignment as a basic principle without even any serious discussion of its relevance for Nepal. Second, Kathmandu accepted a client-state role in India's regional security, economic, and political systems. The 1950 treaty the Ranas had signed with India was retained and even expanded. A 1954 joint Indian-Nepali memorandum, for instance, provided for the coordination of foreign policy. The establishment of an Indian military mission in Nepal in 1953 and of Indian posts on Nepal's northern border in 1954 associated Nepal even more directly in India's security system. And an informal system of periodic consultation between top officials of both governments assured a continual exchange of views, thus facilitating New Delhi's guidance of Kathmandu on foreign-policy matters.

While King Tribhuvan was on the throne, the Nepal government cautiously restricted contacts with the outside world to the minimum level acceptable to India. The United States and Great Britain had established formal diplomatic relations with Nepal during the Rana period; these were continued, but on a low-profile basis. In 1951, the United States did establish an economic-aid program in Nepal (which had been negotiated with the Ranas), but it was not until 1958 that an American embassy was finally approved for Kathmandu. Membership in the United Nations presented Nepal with an alternative channel of communications with the outside world, but one that was used very cautiously in the first few years—in effect, Nepal provided India with a second vote in the UN General Assembly. After its conquest of Tibet in 1951, China began to make some friendly overtures to Kathmandu, but with evident deference to India's wishes and interests. Nepal's responses were usually carefully contrived to move in conjunction with or even slightly behind New Delhi. It was only after India had signed a treaty with China on the Tibet question in 1954, for instance, that Kathmandu began to seriously consider the establishment of diplomatic relations with Peking.

The rhetoric on economic development common to most developing countries in the 1950s was widely expressed in Nepal, but in policy terms was interpreted to mean the expansion of economic relations with India. Nepal's economic policy, like its foreign policy, was closely integrated with that of the Indian government, and New Delhi's guidance on such issues was usually the critical factor in Nepali decision making.

The Mahendra Regnum

In 1956, about one year after King Mahendra had come to

the throne, some significant changes in Nepali foreign-policy strategies began to be evident. Perhaps the most important was the reinterpretation given—gradually and rather subtly—to the concept of nonalignment. The Indian definition of nonalignment in global Cold War terms was abandoned for a policy of nonalignment *between India and China*—expressed in the new terminology that emphasized "equal friendship with India and China." Implicitly, at least, this constituted an effort by Nepal to opt out of—or at least reduce—its role in the Indian security system and was interpreted as such by New Delhi. Since these policy initiatives coincided with the emergence of a Sino-Indian border dispute, the Indian response was unequivocal—i.e., changes in the 1950 treaty or 1954 memorandum were not acceptable. Nepal lacked the capacity to force India to agree to modifications in their treaty relationship, but some initial steps were taken with that objective in view.

While Mahendra's efforts to neutralize Nepal were severely constrained by objective conditions, his political and economic-diversification policies directed at decreasing India's role in Nepal were pushed with considerable vigor. These were intended to provide the basis for the eventual termination of the special relationship with India. Political relations were established with a large number of countries and on a different basis than in the past. The United States, Soviet Union, and China all established embassies in Kathmandu in the 1958–1960 period and were followed thereafter by numerous other states from all regions of the world. In one decade, Nepal was transformed from a status as one of the world's most closed societies to that of one of the more accessible of the small states in the Third World. On international issues, Kathmandu also sought to define a position in international agencies, such as the United Nations, that was something other than a follow-the-leader role to India. There have been, of course, powerful political constraints upon Nepal's capacity to do this, for the costs involved may run much higher than any gains that might accrue to Nepal for its independent posture. Thus, although Nepal has voted differently from India in the United Nations on a number of occasions, rarely has this involved issues on which New Delhi's basic interests were involved. The one important exception to this general rule concerns the terms upon which landlocked states should have access to the sea. India and Nepal support basically different positions on this vital issue.

Mahendra's most vigorous and important efforts at diversification were in terms of economic policy, discussed in some detail in Chapter 4. The strategy adopted was to involve as wide a range as possible of states and international agencies in Nepal's economic development, both through aid programs and trade. The basic objective was to lessen Nepal's economic dependence upon India as a supplier of goods and capital and as a market for Nepali products. Until and unless this was achieved, Mahendra argued, there was no real possibility of modifying Nepal's special relationship with India no matter how "independent" the government might be in the rhetoric used on a wide range of issues. He was of course right; but as he later learned through painful experience, this was easier said than done.

The 1962 Sino-Indian border war, which culminated in a humiliating defeat for the Indians on the eastern and western extremes of their long border with China, opened up new policy options for Kathmandu in its relations with both of its giant neighbors. In the summer and fall of 1962, the government of India began to place heavy pressure upon King Mahendra to come to terms with the "democratic" opposition forces in Nepal by applying unofficial economic pressure (e.g., in effect, closing the border to trade through the strict enforcement of bureaucratic technicalities) as well as supporting increased terrorist activities by the rebels. The vulnerability of Nepal to this limited form of intervention became very evident. Mahendra was on the verge of making major concessions when China's initiation of hostilities on its borders with India in October 1962 drastically changed the entire regional environment. In New Delhi, top priority was now given to strengthening India's security system on its northern frontier; one aspect of this policy innovation was a sudden and nearly total turnabout in policy toward Nepal. The Nepali opposition forces operating from support bases inside India were instructed to cease their terrorist activities in Nepal and use peaceful political tactics. India also made a serious effort to improve relations with Mahendra, providing what amounted to an implicit guarantee of the royal regime against India-based opposition forces.

Mahendra was now in a position to attempt to develop a political system based on something more than a desperate struggle for survival. The "partyless" panchayat polity was the eventual consequence.

At least equally important to Mahendra were the concessions extracted from New Delhi in the 1963–1967 period on economic issues. New Delhi reluctantly agreed to several Nepali demands, particularly on transit trade with third countries through India and on access to Indian markets. This allowed Mahendra to push his economic-diversification programs in ways that had seemed inconceivable when they were first introduced in the late 1950s. Kathmandu made the most of this unexpected opportunity by steadily raising the level of its demands on India, more often than not with some success. For a time, almost anything seemed possible and the level of expectations in Nepal on its capacity to extract concessions from India rose accordingly.

Some significant changes in Nepal's informal affiliation with the Indian frontier security system were also achieved in the post-1962 period, although these generally were contrived to meet the interests and demands of both sides. Although the Mahendra regime had benefited substantially from China's "India war," the results had also raised some problems for Kathmandu. China had clearly demonstrated that it was prepared to use military force against neighboring states; and if today India, why not Nepal tomorrow? Moreover, the Chinese victory indicated the lack of a military power balance on the Himalayan frontier, and this ran against the broader Nepali interest in an approximate balance of power between its two powerful and dangerous neighbors. Something had to be done. In the 1963–1965 period, New Delhi agreed to suspend the arrangement under which India provided Nepal its sole source of military supply, and Kathmandu was permitted to purchase a limited amount of arms and military equipment from the United States and Britain in order to improve the capacity of the Nepali army both to assure internal stability and to resist external intervention. In 1965, however, a secret agreement was reached between India and Nepal under which the latter agreed to return to the earlier arrangement under which it obtained all military equipment from India. This met New Delhi's interest in a monopoly on arms sales to Nepal, but it also served to guarantee Indian support of the Nepali royal regime.

During the 1969–1970 period, developments in Indo-Nepali security-system relations once again began to move in new and dangerous directions. Suddenly and unexpectedly in 1969, Prime Minister Kirtinidhi Bista demanded the withdrawal of both the Indian military mission that had operated out of the Nepal-army headquarters in Kathmandu since 1953 and the Indian military personnel stationed at Nepal's northern border posts. New Delhi finally acceded to the demand, but with the determination to make Nepal pay highly for this concession. The delays in the conclusion of a new trade and transit treaty in 1970, at the time stipulated in the 1960 treaty, was one consequence—and an extremely expensive one economically for Nepal. Eventually, a new treaty was signed in 1971, but on somewhat less generous terms than the 1960 agreement. Coincidentally, India was allowed to attach a military mission to its embassy staff in Kathmandu. Although it no longer operated out of Nepal's military headquarters, its relations with the head-quarters staff were and still are reportedly very close.

While all these changes were taking place in Indo-Nepali relations in the post-1962 period, Kathmandu moved to expand its ties with China in a cautious, carefully defined manner. As noted above, it was not considered to be in Nepal's interests to allow China to expand its involvement in Nepal in ways that would undermine the Indian security system, which, after all, is the only effective protection that Nepal has against the Chinese. Although the government in Kathmandu is reasonably certain that Peking will not intervene in Nepal either directly or through assistance to a revolutionary movement against the royal regime as long as India constitutes an effective counter-balance to Chinese power, it is less confident that this would be the case if India were severely weakened. Thus, keeping both neighbors involved in Nepal, but in ways that contribute to the stability of the existing political system, is still the basic objective of Nepali foreign policy.

China's involvement in Nepal has generally conformed to Kathmandu's expectations, but there have been a few exceptions. Nepal's agreement to allow China to build a road connecting Kathmandu with the Tibet border, for instance, was announced by King Mahendra in late 1961 when relations with India were deteriorating rapidly and some form of tangible support from Peking seemed necessary. While the Kathmandu authorities lauded this "achievement" of Nepali foreign policy, they also realized that the road posed a potential security problem for Nepal (and India). It then constituted the only road that breached the Himalayan barrier. There was also the system under which China provided limited financial assistance to some ostensibly pro-Chinese "radical" organizations and political activists through such bodies as the Nepal-China Friendship Society. So far, the Chinese have used their assistance to such groups to moderate their opposition to the political system, producing a "royalist" Communist faction in the process. But as the royal regime knows, China could use this support system for oppositional purposes under different sets of circumstances.

There were, in any case, great expectations in Nepal throughout the 1960s concerning the benefits to be derived from the China connection; it seemed to provide the political and military environment in the Himalayan region that made Kathmandu's neutralization and diversification policies feasible. For a time, at least, it lessened Nepal's vulnerability to Indian pressure without—and this was important to Mahendra—substantially expanding China's capacity to exert influence on the royal regime. The balance-the-powers game became increasingly attractive and was indulged in with fervor and enthusiasm. The relationship with China also promised to add substance to Nepal's economic-diversification policy. The road to Tibet, it was hoped, would provide Nepal with an alternative to Calcutta for its transit trade, in the process reducing the economic and political liabilities associated with Nepal's status as a landlocked country. There was also a substantial expansion of the amount of foreign aid available in the post-1962 period, which was, in part, a reflection of Nepal's geostrategic role in the Sino-Indian dispute. Both India and China substantially increased their aid contributions, but the United States and the Soviet Union did likewise as part of their support-the-Indians policy in this period. Here also, Nepal encouraged an atmosphere of competition and discouraged any forms of cooperation among aid donors in order to increase aid and provide the royal regime with broader controls over its use.[1]

By the beginning of the 1970s there appeared to be a more realistic appraisal in Kathmandu of the inevitable limitations on the use of the "China card." The substantial expansion of the Indian military in the post-1962 period—from approximately 500,000 to a million men—was one factor. The balance of military power on the Himalayan border shifted gradually to India's favor, leading eventually to a probable Indian superiority at key points on the frontier. Thus, Nepal ended up about as vulnerable to Indian pressure in the 1970s as it had been before the 1962 Sino-Indian war. There was, moreover, considerable resentment in Indian government circles over the tactics Nepal had employed to extract concessions during periods of Indian weakness, as well as a strong determination to change the process of interaction between the two states. The hard-line positions adopted by the Indian government in most negotiations with Nepal since 1970 have been, in part, a reflection of this attitude, and Kathmandu has found the China connection of limited utility under these changed circumstances.

Nepal also made disappointing progress in the implementation of its economic-diversification program. China never developed as an alternative market or transit channel for Nepal, and the Kathmandu-Tibet road has proved to be not only expensive to maintain but virtually useless in economic terms. Diversification brought in much more foreign aid, but there were increasing doubts in Kathmandu about its contribution to Nepal's economic development. There was too much duplication of efforts and too little coordination among the aid donors, some Nepalis argued. This made the formulation of a rational economic-development program a near impossibility, for the Nepalis responsible for economic planning and allocation of resources had only limited control over development budgets. The need to integrate the foreign-aid programs into a Nepali-devised economic-development program was stressed, but this, of course, ran directly against Kathmandu's political policy of encouraging competition and discouraging cooperation among the aid donors. A basic change in policy obviously required was not easily achieved, and the Mahendra period ended without a broad consensus on these issues among the decision-making elites and institutions responsible for the formulation of foreign policy.

The Birendra Period

The death of King Mahendra in January 1972 brought the young Crown Prince Birendra Bir Bikram Shah Dev to the throne. The new king had been gradually inducted into the process of decision making by his father over the previous two years and thus had been reasonably well socialized into the political system and policies of the Mahendra regnum. Birendra, however, was not enthusiastic about some aspects of the Mahendra system; moreover, he had also undergone a variety of educational experiences in India, Great Britain, the United States, and Japan that had exposed him to intellectual cross currents in the outside world, an opportunity denied to King Mahendra in his youth by the Rana-regime policy of isolating the royal family. In this period, Birendra had established close personal relations with a number of young, highly educated, and talented Nepalis, several of whom had earned doctorates from foreign universities in different fields in the social sciences. Thus, from the beginning of his reign, Birendra was surrounded by very different types of advisers and consultants from the group of older, mostly high-level government servants who had served in this capacity in the latter years of Mahendra's reign.

The change in political style and in the character of palace cliques in the new regnum inevitably affected policy issues as Birendra sought to establish an image distinct from that of his father. In foreign policy, however, the change was more rhetorical, as the basic objectives of his predecessor were retained and even strengthened. Mahendra's efforts to neutralize Nepal, somewhat muted in the last years of his reign, were reinvigorated by his successor. Indeed, not long after ascending the throne, Birendra issued a statement in which Nepal's status as a south Asian state was questioned, a subtle attempt to further dissociate the country from the region that was, following the Indo-Pakistani war of 1971, more dominated by India than at any time since 1947. New Delhi quietly indicated its displeasure with this geopolitical adjustment of regional boundaries, and similar statements were not repeated subsequently by the king or other Nepali officials. But this was indicative of the direction in which Birendra hoped to move Nepal's relations with the outside world.

The major effort to provide greater substance to the neutralization policy was introduced by King Birendra at the 1973 nonaligned conference in Algeria when he stated that "Nepal, situated between two of the most populous countries in the world, wishes within her frontiers to be declared a zone of peace." None of the other delegates at the conference commented one way or the other on this unique proposal to make a particular country a "zone of peace," and nothing more was heard on the subject for nearly two years. Then, in his coronation address on February 25, 1975, Birendra specifically asked neighboring states and other powers to formally recognize Nepal as a zone of peace. This subsequently has become the major theme in Nepali foreign-policy statements. Although this obviously serves to further the neutralization objective, Kathmandu has been less than clear in defining the steps other than a formal recognition that would be required to make its zone-of-peace status a reality. By necessity, it would seem, the 1950 Indo-Nepali treaty would have to be abrogated or at least substantially amended, and some of the other less public agreements with India (e.g., the 1965 agreement on the supply of military equipment) would not fit easily into this new format.

The response from other powers has been what one would expect. Most of the nonregional powers, including the United States and the Soviet Union, maintain a position characterized by ambiguity; they do not want to reject the zone-of-peace proposal publicly, but neither will attach its name to any such document until India has done so. China, Pakistan, and Bangladesh quickly endorsed the proposal when asked to do so by Kathmandu in 1976 and have stated their willingness to sign an international document on this basis. But, if Nepal is expecting these states to take the initiative in pressing this subject in international forums, it may once again be disappointed.

The critical response for Nepal, of course, was that of

India, since New Delhi's nonadherence would make a zone-of-peace agreement endorsed by the rest of the world a scrap of paper. And the Indian position on this issue was made perfectly clear by both the Indira Gandhi and the Morarji Desai governments—namely, that New Delhi will not buy it in any form, shape, or definition. The usual Indian approach is to blithely dismiss the proposal that Nepal be declared a zone of peace by stating that it is India's objective to have the whole of south Asia—or sometimes Asia or the world—declared a zone of peace. This amounts to a rejection of the proposal, although it is not stated in that way, and the rejection is further strengthened by frequently reiterated statements that India considers the 1950 Indo-Nepali treaty to still be in force in all its aspects, without need of revision or abrogation. The prospects, thus, for the declaration of Nepal as a zone of peace do not seem very hopeful, for this would require a basic change in Indian policy.

In the economic sphere, the Birendra regime sought to expand and revitalize the diversification program introduced by Mahendra but gradually modified in the last years of his reign. Key members of Birendra's new clique of advisers did not share the drastic revision downward in expectations of economic benefits from the China connection that had been reluctantly accepted by Mahendra's inner circle following the extensive and traumatic renegotiation of the trade treaty with India in 1971. This group of well-educated but mostly inexperienced young men had constructed their theories on foreign policy in the halcyon days of the mid-1960s when the use of the China card had seemingly paid handsome dividends for Nepal and were largely unaware of the increasingly heavy price Nepal had to pay for these accomplishments a few years later. They were, in any case, reluctant to accept the view that times and circumstances had changed and that policies had to be adjusted accordingly.

The consequence was a serious, if largely nonpublic, worsening of relations between Nepal and India in the 1972–1977 period. A number of developments contributed to this trend. The official encouragement given to the "popular" demonstrations in Kathmandu in 1973, protesting the Indian actions in Sikkim that set the stage for the accession of that border state into the Indian republic, brought a strong protest from New Delhi, accompanied once again by economic pressure upon Nepal through the use of trade-control technicalities. The Nepal government was silent on this issue thereafter, even in 1975 when Sikkim was absorbed by India, but its great concern over this development was readily evident. The Nepali view of Mrs. Gandhi as a leader who preferred to meet crisis situations by resorting to ultimate options without exploring less forceful responses, graphically demonstrated during the 1971 Indo-Pakistani war over Bangladesh, was reinforced by the events in Sikkim. New Delhi's assurances that this was not a precedent for Indian policy toward other border states was received with some skepticism in Kathmandu, but also with a growing awareness in the palace of Nepal's vulnerability.

In 1974, the Nepal government found itself in a position to undertake a police action—using the Nepal army—directed at the Tibetan (Khampa) refugee centers in the northern border regions that, in practice, controlled some sections of Nepali territory on the border with Tibet. Kathmandu had never reconciled itself to this situation but previously had lacked the capacity to do much about it despite the periodic complaints from China that these Tibetans were raiding across the border into Tibet. Serious divisions within the Khampa rebel forces in 1974 provided Nepal with the opportunity to bring these sensitive frontier areas back under effective control, and the operation was launched. Peking applauded, of course, but New Delhi, which had been providing material and financial assistance to the Tibetans since the 1962 Sino-Indian war (reportedly with the cooperation of the United States prior to 1971 and with the Soviets thereafter), was less than happy as this trumped one of their high cards in the long process of negotiations with China on their Himalayan border. If the Khampas were to be brought under control, the Indians preferred to do this as a concession to China in exchange for a concession—perhaps the termination of Chinese support for Naga and Mizo rebels in northeastern India.

A number of other events, including King Birendra's highly publicized visit to Szechwan and Tibet provinces in China in

1976—just prior to a new round of negotiations on the Nepal-India trade and transit treaty—were not particularly important in themselves but contributed to a steady if undramatic deterioration in Indo-Nepali relations. The Indian response was by now classic—the use of delay tactics in the renegotiation of the 1971 trade and transit treaty that was due to expire in 1976. In this instance, New Delhi even threatened to discontinue applying the terms of the 1971 treaty on an ad hoc basis until a new agreement was concluded, which would have been an instant disaster for the Nepali economy. The Indians eventually backed down unofficially on this issue but did introduce some other changes in Indo-Nepali economic relations that were expensive to Nepal.

By 1977, there appeared to be increasing sophistication in the Birendra regime concerning trends in foreign policy, particularly with respect to the strategies employed in dealing with India. A number of factors contributed to this modest change in perspective. The defeat of Mrs. Gandhi and the Congress party in the March 1977 election in India was generally welcomed in Kathmandu, though not without some reservations. Although Mrs. Gandhi had adopted an increasingly hard line on political and economic relations with Nepal (e.g., the trade and transit treaty), she had also dissociated her government from the Nepali oppositionist forces based in India and had applied ever sharper restrictions on their operations. The situation had become so difficult for the Nepali exiles that the principal leader, B. P. Koirala, had decided to return to Nepal in December 1976—three months before Mrs. Gandhi's unexpected electoral defeat—without having extracted any concessions from the royal regime that immediately imprisoned him again. The new Janata government, on the other hand, included a number of old Socialist party leaders who had had a long relationship with Koirala and other Nepali oppositionist leaders, and this aroused considerable concern in the palace as to the policy of the new Indian government toward the royal regime in Nepal. Fortunately for King Birendra and his closest consultants, the Janata government, and particularly Foreign Minister A. B. Vaypayee, moved quickly to reassure Kathmandu on this matter by projecting a more open and responsive position on the critical issues dividing the two states. New Delhi has taken a series of steps, mostly minor but indicative of a new approach, designed to placate Nepal, and in fact the Janata government proved to be no more supportive of the Nepali opposition than its predecessor despite some unofficial endorsements by Janata leaders.

The bona fides of the Janata government in its expressed desire to improve the basis of its relationship with all neighboring states, including Nepal, was fairly widely accepted in Kathmandu, though of course with some reservations. The result has been a spasmodic but still significant improvement in Indo-Nepali relations in the late 1970s and some new policy initiatives from both sides. These were most evident, perhaps, in the new treaties of trade and transit signed in 1978. New Delhi finally accepted the Nepali demand for separate treaties on these two subjects and also liberalized the terms of both in some respects. But in most respects, the new treaties reflect the basic positions of the Indian government, and New Delhi is quite satisfied that the agreements serve India's economic, political, and regional interests. In 1978, one subsequent policy innovation in Nepal, which derives logically from the new treaty and also meets a long-standing demand by India, was the modification of the system under which Nepali trade with third countries was used extensively to support the large-scale smuggling of commodities between India and Nepal. Although the new policy will not totally prevent this intricate smuggling system, it will probably meet India's minimum demands.

But even more indicative of the improvement in Indo-Nepali relations, with potential long-range implications for Nepal's domestic and international economic policy, was the agreement in 1978 on joint ventures between Indian and Nepali firms in industrial spheres. This could provide the basis for a substantial expansion of Indian investment in Nepal as well as a significant change in the type of Indian firms that might be involved. Previously, the Nepal government had, in effect, discouraged investment by the larger, more reputable Indian firms because of its concern that this would magnify even further Indian domination of the Nepali economy. Most of the Indian investors in Nepal had been comparatively small-scale operatives, more interested in the possibilities for large and quick profits than in contributing to the development of industries that operated on a more long-term basis. The "quick-rupee" investors had demonstrated considerable initiative at times in their operations in Nepal and had contributed to the economic well-being of a number of Nepali government servants and other elites, but had made little positive contribution to real economic development in Nepal.

It is hoped that the new agreement will change this situation and that India will now contribute in significant ways to industrial and commercial development in Nepal. But the royal regime has had to make substantial modifications in its own policies, not only with respect to the terms upon which Indian firms invest in Nepal, but more basically with respect to its economic-diversification policy. If the joint project programs reach anything like the proportions envisaged in the 1978 agreement, it is inevitable that Nepal's economy and foreign trade will be interrelated with those of India to an even greater extent than at present. To some Nepalis, this is most dangerous and unfortunate and threatens to transform their country into a dependent state. Others argue that this is already the case and that Nepal will benefit from this new arrangement by achieving something that has avoided its grasp through the application of the diversification program—namely, a positive rate of economic development. The debate on this subject is certain to become more intense when (and if) the consequences of the joint venture agreement become more evident.

International Factors in Decision Making in Nepal

It is a normal phenomenon for the foreign policy of any society to be strongly affected by domestic political and economic factors, and this is certainly the case in Nepal. But the reverse principle—namely, that international factors have a strong and often decisive impact on Kathmandu's domestic policies—is even more apparent. This is a painful fact of life for many Nepalis, and one that some of them would prefer to ignore. But despite intensive efforts over several centuries to isolate the country from alien influences of all kinds and to emphasize indigenous responses to new situations and challenges, the penetration of Nepal from outside is truly massive in scale and probably irreversible.

As we have already noted, the consequences of such penetration are readily apparent in virtually all aspects of Nepali society. The intellectuals trained in India and the West who dominate policymaking, bureaucratic, and educational institutions endeavor to design policies and programs that are based on Nepali values, but the imprint of their exposure to prevailing international concepts and models is evident. Skepticism about the advice received from foreign aid and UN missions in Kathmandu is now expressed in fairly strong language. But, in fact, the Nepali elite's perception of issues and solutions does not vary significantly from those of the "outsiders" since both groups are, after all, the products of a common educational and intellectual socialization.

Cultural and value-related penetration below the elite level may not be as pervasive, but it is increasingly significant. Even the most isolated areas of the country are now exposed to multiple sources of external influences, including the omnipresence of transistor radios. The radio audience in Nepal, moreover, has a wide range of choices of Nepali language broadcasts from such diverse sources as Radio Lhasa (Chinese), All-India Radio, the BBC, and the Voice of America, in addition to Radio Nepal. Thus it is almost impossible for anything that happens in Nepal to be kept secret from the Nepali public through governmental controls over the media. While the Nepali press can be "guided" with reasonable efficiency by the authorities,[2] there is no way in which the uncontrolled Indian press can be excluded from the country—and in particular from the Kathmandu valley and the Tarai, the most politicized areas of the country—for any extended period.

The susceptibility of Nepal to the influence of international factors is also evident in other, more specific ways on the media question. It was by no means coincidental, for instance, that a 1976 Nepal government ordinance applied stricter controls over the press than ever before, using virtually the same language as that employed shortly before by Mrs. Gandhi's emergency regime in imposing tight restrictions on the press in India. The general principle seemed to be that as long as India had a free press, there were some implicit limits upon what the Nepal government could do (in legislative terms, at least) to manage the Nepal press. But once an authoritarian Indian government moved to bring its own press under control, the Nepal government could, and did, follow suit. Although Kathmandu did not emulate the Janata government in India by repealing its press act in 1977, the rules have been applied more liberally in Nepal, in particular since the King's announcement of a national referendum in May 1979.

Nepal's vulnerability to external economic forces and its dependence upon foreign aid have already been discussed at length, and there is no need to go into this again. But here as well international factors have had a major impact upon decision making within the Nepal government and upon the responses of critical political elites to a wide range of policy decisions. One can only sympathize with those who are responsible for the definition of policies and strategies under such circumstances, as well as admire the imagination and determination with which they have sought to manipulate an extremely difficult international environment to serve Nepali purposes and goals. That they have had only limited success in this endeavor over the long run is perhaps inevitable, but here also their capacity for adjustment to new, often distressing realities deserves respect. A significant diminution in foreign penetration and influence in the foreseeable future does not seem probable; indeed, the opposite may be more likely. Given its track record, however, it is reasonable to assume that Kathmandu will continue to function as an independent-minded, fiercely nationalistic polity that exploits any and all opportunities to devise policies that advance its perceptions of Nepal's interests.

Notes

1. Nepali adroitness in the exploitation of foreign-aid programs in the mid-1960s was amply demonstrated in the field of road construction. King Mahendra had defined the construction of an east-west highway traversing the country as a major objective shortly after his dismissal

of the Nepali Congress government in December 1961. He approached India and the United States for support in this massive and, for Nepal, very expensive project, but neither government indicated any interest in getting involved. Kathmandu then began negotiating with China for the construction of a road that would connect the Kathmandu-Tibet highway with the Tarai, thus involving Chinese in road construction (and related) activities in areas near the Nepal-India border. Both India and the United States objected strongly to Kathmandu. King Mahendra then informed the Chinese that their road project was being canceled and persuaded them instead to undertake responsibility for the Kathmandu-Pokhara road! At the same time, he extracted agreements from both India and the United States to construct substantial sections of his east-west highway in exchange for his compliance with their "advice" on the Chinese road.

2. The "guided" Nepali press is very skilled at transmitting prescribed information to its alert public. One common practice, for instance, is to denounce in the strongest language possible either a statement by an opposition leader or some antigovernment event. A newspaper can thereby bring the subject to the attention of the public—but in a way that makes the government look ridiculous if it takes action against the paper. There are limits on this, of course, and it is not uncommon for a paper to be banned for a period of time for exceeding the loosely defined boundaries on news reporting.

Suggested Books on Nepal

An excellent collection of articles on various aspects of Nepal by Nepali scholars is contained in Pashupati Shumshere J. B. Rana and Kamal P. Malla (eds.) *Nepal in Perspective* (Kathmandu: Centre for Economic Development and Administration, 1973). For a more extensive overview of Nepal, see Rishikesh Shaha, *An Introduction to Nepal* (Kathmandu: Ratna Pustak Bhandar, 1976). The best general book on Nepal's geography is still Toni Hagan, Friedrich T. Wahlen, and Walter R. Corti, *Nepal: The Kingdom in the Himalaya* (Berne: Kümmerly Frey, 1961). An introduction to religious festivals can be found in Mary M. Anderson, *The Festivals of Nepal* (London: George Allen, 1971). The most thorough bibliography is L. Boulnois and H. Millot, *Bibliographie du Népal* (Paris: Centre National de la Recherche Scientifique, 1969); and the 1975 *Supplément* by L. Boulnois.

The most prolific Nepali writer on historical topics has been Dilli Raman Regmi, who has written, among other things, *Ancient Nepal* (Calcutta: Firma K. L. Mukhopadhyay, 1969), *Medieval Nepal,* 3 vols. (Calcutta: Firma K. L. Mukhopadhyay, 1965-66), and *Modern Nepal* (Calcutta: Firma K. L. Mukhopadhyay, 1961). For a detailed account of Nepal's unification and the immediate aftermath, see Ludwig F. Stiller, *The Rise of the House of Gorkha* (Patna: Jesuit Society, 1973), and his follow-up study, *The Silent Cry: The People of Nepal: 1816-39* (Kathmandu: Sahayogi Press, 1976). For an account of economic history, see the writings of Mahesh C. Regmi, such as *A Study in Economic History: 1768-1846* (New Delhi: Manjusri Publishing House, 1971) and *Thatched Huts and Stucco Palaces: Peasant and Landlord in Nineteenth Century Nepal* (New Delhi: Vikas, 1978).

A general introduction to Nepal's political institutions can be found in Leo E. Rose and Margaret W. Fisher, *The Politics of Nepal: Persistence and Change in an Asian Monarchy* (Ithaca, N.Y.: Cornell

University Press, 1970). A good collection of essays on a wide range of political topics is contained in S. D. Muni (ed.), *Nepal: An Assertive Monarchy* (New Delhi: Chetana Publications, 1977). The 1950s and early 1960s have been studied in Bhuwan Lal Joshi and Leo E. Rose, *Democratic Innovations in Nepal* (Berkeley and Los Angeles: University of California Press, 1966); Anirudha Gupta, *Politics in Nepal* (Bombay: Allied Publishers, 1964); and R. S. Chauhan, *The Political Development in Nepal, 1950–1970* (New Delhi: Associated, 1971). More current accounts can be found in Rishikesh Shaha, *Nepali Politics: Retrospect and Prospect* (Delhi: Oxford University Press, 1975); and Tribhuvan Nath, *The Nepalese Dilemma* (New Delhi: Sterling Publishers, 1975). Two good books on more specialized subjects are Frederick H. Gaige, *Regionalism and National Unity in Nepal* (Berkeley and Los Angeles: University of California Press, 1975); and Lok Raj Baral, *Oppositional Politics in Nepal* (Columbia, Mo.: South Asia Books [1978]). For a detailed account of Nepal's administrative institutions, see Hem Narayan Agrawal, *The Administrative System of Nepal: From Tradition to Modernity* (New Delhi: Vikas, 1976); Nanda Lall Joshi, *Evolution of Public Administration in Nepal* (Kathmandu: Centre for Economic Development and Administration, 1973); and Mangal Krishna Shrestha, *Public Administration in Nepal* (Kathmandu: Educational Enterprise, 1975).

Dor Bahadur Bista, *Peoples of Nepal* (Kathmandu: Ratna Pustak Bhandar, 1967), remains the best general reference on the cultures of Nepal's numerous ethnic groups. A more recent collection of essays on various groups and topics can be found in Christoph von Fürer-Haimendorf (ed.), *Contributions to the Anthropology of Nepal* (Warminster, Pa.: Aris and Phillips, 1974). Many good monographs deal with particular ethnic groups or areas, such as John T. Hitchcock, *The Magars of Banyan Hill* (New York: Holt, 1966); Rex L. Jones and Shirley Kurz Jones, *The Himalayan Woman: A Study of Limbu Women in Marriage and Divorce* (Palo Alto, Calif.: Mayfield, 1976); Donald A. Messerschmidt, *The Gurungs of Nepal* (Warminster, Pa.: Aris and Phillips, 1976); Christoph von Fürer-Haimendorf, *Himalayan Traders* (New York: St. Martin's, 1975); Gopal Singh Nepali, *The Newars: An Ethno-Sociological Study of a Himalayan Community* (Bombay: United Asia Publications, 1965); Lionel Caplan, *Land and Social Change in East Nepal: A Study of Hindu-Tribal Relations* (Berkeley and Los Angeles: University of California Press, 1970), and his more recent *Administration and Politics in a Nepalese Town: The Study of a District Capital and Its Environs* (London: Oxford University Press, 1975); and Patricia A. Caplan, *Priests and Cobblers: A Study of Social Change in a Hindu Village in Western Nepal* (San Francisco, Calif.: Chandler, 1972). Shamanism in different groups and regions is discussed in

John T. Hitchcock and Rex Jones, *Spirit Possession in the Nepal Himalayas* (Warminster, Pa.: Aris and Phillips, 1976). Numerous Ph.D. dissertations on Nepal have been written in recent years and provide the most current studies on anthropological subjects. Current dissertations are listed occasionally in the *Bulletin* of the Nepal Studies Association, published three times annually in the United States.

For a general overview of the economy see Badri Prasad Shrestha, *An Introduction to the Nepalese Economy* (Kathmandu: Ratna Pustak Bhandar, 1974). More specialized studies can be found in Yadav Prasad Pant and S. C. Jain, *Agricultural Development in Nepal* (Bombay: Vora, 1969); Charles McDougal, *Village and Household Economy in Far Western Nepal* (Kirtipur, Nepal: Tribhuvan University, 1968); Mahesh Chandra Regmi, *Landownership in Nepal* (Berkeley and Los Angeles: University of California Press, 1974); John Beyer, *Budget Innovations in Developing Countries: The Experience of Nepal* (New York: Praeger, 1973); M. A. Zaman, *An Evaluation of Land Reform in Nepal* (Kathmandu: Ministry of Land Reform, 1973); and David Seddon (ed.), *Peasants and Workers in Nepal: The Conditions of the Lower Classes* (Warminster, Pa.: Aris and Phillips, 1978).

The most comprehensive study of Nepal's international relations is Leo E. Rose, *Nepal: Strategy for Survival* (Berkeley and Los Angeles: University of California Press, 1971). More specialized studies of Nepal's foreign policy include S. D. Muni, *Foreign Policy of Nepal* (New Delhi: National, 1973); K. Mojumdar, *Political Relations between India and Nepal 1877-1923* (New Delhi: Munshiram Manoharlal, 1973); P. C. Rawat, *Indo-Nepal Economic Relations* (New Delhi: National, 1974); and Ramakant, *Nepal—China and India* (New Delhi: Abhinav, 1976).

Index

143